HORSES
AT WORK

HORSES
AT WORK

DONALD J. SMITH

 Patrick Stephens, Wellingborough

Title spread *Three horse unicorn rig of Percherons* (Robert A. Smith).

First published in 1985

British Library Cataloguing in Publication Data

Smith, D. J.
  Horses at work
  1. Draft horses
  I. Title
  636.1'5   SF311

  ISBN 0-85059-737-4

Patrick Stephens Limited is part of the Thorsons Publishing Group

Photoset in 11 on 12 pt Baskerville by J & L Composition Ltd, Filey, North Yorks. Printed in Great Britain on 120 gsm Clandon Matt coated cartridge, and bound by Butler & Tanner Limited, Frome, Somerset, for the publishers, Patrick Stephens Limited, Denington Estate, Wellingborough, Northants, NN8 2QD, England.

Contents

Introduction

Prophets of doom foretold the premature extinction of the working horse from the second half of the 18th century and introduction of steam power as a viable means of locomotion. Yet neither railways nor mechanically-powered road vehicles were to become a universal reality until well into the following century, while horseless carriages only began to dominate the scene during the 1930s. Although it was frequently claimed that horses were no longer the animals of the future, especially for draught and burden, they served a long interim period in primary and secondary roles, especially delivering goods and cultivating crops. While steam railways dashed passengers and goods from centre-to-centre at over a mile a minute, most people were taken to the station in horse cabs or buses, while all merchandise from small packages to huge castings trundled from railhead and goods depot on wagon or dray.

On the farm horses were, for many years, part of a way of life. This continued at least until the middle of the Great War when, as a result of so many horses being needed to pull guns and supply wagons, Lloyd-George had to appeal to America for emergency shipments of Fordson tractors. This may be seen as a turning point and the demand to mechanise rapidly dominated the thoughts of more progressive farmers and businessmen, the least sentimental — by their own standards — being the most gullible to the wiles of trained salesmen and publicists. By the mid-1930s wholesale mechanisation of the army, agriculture and industry was well under way, halted only by the outbreak of the Second World War, when some of the remaining horse-owners were encouraged to keep their animals, if only to save imported fuel for tanks and lorries, without which the British and Allied armies would have been unable to take the field. The situation of the First World War was reversed — the nation was nearly immobilised through lack of petrol rather than horse-power. Fortunately there were still many farmers and large concerns, both in industry and transport, who had retained faith in draught horses. The London, Midland and Scottish Railway was even planning to increase its stud well into the 1940s. Yet war-time needs and measures were only temporary, lasting as long as the emergency period and ensuing years of recovery.

With the end of petrol rationing and revival of popular motoring horses were once more pensioned-off and their numbers dropped to alarmingly low levels. A few breeds became extinct and more would have followed but for the interest of enthusiasts and far-sighted people in all walks of life, from royal palace to humble

Cider mill.

croft. Yet the scientific investigations of conservationists and work-study experts have more than justified keeping faith with the horse. During the late 1960s and early 1970s more intelligent theorists were deploring over-mechanisation, while unspoken doubts may have caused a few to wonder if our fragile economic structure was not, at least partly, due to rushing too far and too fast into a brave new world of total technology. There were, and still are, many jobs that can be done as well, if not better, by horses as by machines.

The Americans, astute as ever in matters of finance and economics, were among the first to perceive these truths and from the early 1970s numbers of working horses began to rapidly increase, especially on the farms and agricultural holdings of North America. In Britain some large firms and many individuals came to realise that for short-haul deliveries, within a radius of four miles, horses were much cheaper than any form of mechanical transport, while the publicity and sheer eye-catching delight of horses in action was an advertisement of great value.

It is intended, within the following pages, to record something of this resurgence of interest in the working horse and its place in every-day life. The accent is upon horses kept not so much for sporting events or leisure purposes, mainly

Clydesdale mare.

concerning individual interests, but concentrating on those earning a living in the truly workmanlike sense of the word. It would split hairs to argue the necessity for healthy relaxation and the desirability for young people to learn to care for ponies and treat them as family pets, and that racing, hunting, eventing and showing all have their niche in the scheme of things. While the future seems fully assured for sporting and show animals the position of the working horse, although at present healthy, is less secure beyond the immediate future. It is a subject worthy of examination, never losing sight of how much may depend on trust, understanding and the right blend of enthusiasm. Horses, in the commercial sphere, can only be said to pay their way if they are treated properly and used to their best advantage. Where losses rather than profits are incurred this is frequently due to lack of foresight or elementary common sense, prosaic enough virtues but essentially bound-up with the will to achieve.

It is unthinkable in the modern world that horses, or any form of animal transport, would ever take over from machines. Yet it should be acknowledged that in the most efficient systems there must be contributions from all available talents and resources. Any number of calamities might return the civilised world to conditions of a new stone age, in which the use of animal power, if only as a temporary measure, would be essential for recovery. Apart from practical matters concerning the present, it is wise strategy to keep open as many options as possible.

In choosing examples to represent the community of working horses, there are bound to be borderline cases and anomalies. Horses used for ceremonial purposes are included, also horses in entertainment. At some point a division has to be made and I felt that the dignity and symbolism of state ceremonial was on an entirely different plane from showing in the ring or training horses to win cups over jumps or on a race track. The need for such display at a national level may be arguable but it exists and is recognised by many as a meaningful reality. Popular entertainments with a mass appeal are also essential to the mental well-being of most people — an area including films, television, theatre and circus, all developing from a common source, not only as a passing delight but forms of self-expression and artistry. This is not to deny honours to the sporting horse or the show horse and their many supporters, but merely to explain how and why a selective choice has been made.

Acknowledgements

The author wishes to thank the following for help in compiling this book: Abels of East Anglia; J. A. Adnams; E. J. Anderton; The Armed Forces Attache, The French Embassy; K. Atkinson, Farm Manager, St Crispin's Hospital, Northampton; C. Bartholomew, Joint Managing Director, Wadworth and Co Ltd; Robert S. Battersby FTS, FIM, ENT, Blackpool Corporation; Centre Director, US Information Service; Sally Chipperfield's Circus; The Circus Fans Association; James Club; The Coalite Group; Mr and Mrs L. Colloby; The Cromford Canal Society Ltd; George Davis, Press Officer, Whitbread's Brewery; Staff of Walt Disney Productions Ltd; B. Dolan; I. P. Field, Honorary Secretary, Essex Tradesmen's Show; C. A. Flower, Devon Shire Horse Centre; Captain N. J. Foster RHA; Colin Fry; John Frazer, Secretary of The Clydesdale Horse Society; W. Gibb, Transport Manager, Borough of Douglas, IOM; T. Gibson, The Shire Horse Society; The Greater London Horse Show Society; P. M. Green; Chief Inspector Hanna; Michael Hardman, Young and Co's Brewery, Wandsworth; Edward Hart; Editor and staff of *Horse and Driving*; Staff of *Horse and Rider*; The Imperial War Museum; David Jamieson; B. Jones, Assistant Head of Publicity, Lloyds Bank; J. D. Kay; Editor and staff of *The Lady*; London Transport; Lonsdale Advertising Agencies Ltd; R. M. Lucas, Manager, Courage Shire Horse Centre; J. Mantle, Public Relations Officer, Colman's of Norwich; D. G. Maskell, The British Percheron Horse Society; Mary May; F. Meadow; Bill Meadows; The Officer Commanding and staff of the Melton Mowbray Depot RAVC; J. R. Moss MIPM, MBIM, The Riding for the Disabled Association; The Society of Ploughmen; D. Pollard; L. D. Pugh; Richard Read, Secretary of the Southern Counties Heavy Horse Society; Rothmans of Pall Mall; Staff of the Royal Mews; Philip Ryder-Davies MB, BS, BVSc, MRVS, Secretary of The Suffolk Horse Society; Robert A. Smith (especially for permission to use information concerning the Vaux Breweries); Samuel Smiths Old Brewery, Tadcaster; The Solid Fuel Advisory Service; Simon Stoker; Staff of the Swedish Embassy; Joshua Tetley and Son Ltd; Staff of Daniel Thwaites' Star Brewery; Vaux' Brewery, Sunderland; Colin Waite; Welsh Horse Drawn Holidays; West Country Wildlife Centre, Cricket St Thomas; Officers and staff of the West Midlands Police; White Horse Distilleries; Wight Horse Drawn Caravans; Maj the Rev P. A. Wright MBE.

Chapter 1

State ceremonial

The Royal Mews

Most of the countries that are still monarchies retain their royal stables and carriage processions, although some of the smaller kingdoms, including Nepal and Sikkim, frequently hire horses and carriages for ceremonial from neighbouring states. For making a picturesque impression the horse is unrivalled and Great Britain, with its almost unbroken records of both royal heritage and quality horse breeding, offers some of the most lavish spectacles in the modern world, especially in London. Coronations, jubilees, royal weddings and the State Opening of Parliament attract crowds of loyal citizens from all parts of the country and Commonwealth, making such occasions not only a focus for traditional values but also a boost to the important tourist industry.

Nearly all the reigning families of Great Britain, including the Lord Protector Oliver Cromwell, were devoted to horses. They rode and drove both for health and pleasure and also in state ceremonial. The enthusiasm of the present Queen and her family for such matters is proverbial, forming part of a lively tradition. It is mainly due to the interest of HRH The Duke of Edinburgh that Britain has become a leading exponent of cross-country carriage driving in competitive events, that vie for interest and excitement with the mounted horse trials in which Princess Anne and Captain Mark Phillips have been pre-eminent. Horses are kept at various royal residences from Windsor to Balmoral, with the majority of riding horses at Windsor — the latter including many presented by foreign rulers and governments over a number of years. Most of the horses used in state ceremonial and for drawing coaches or carriages are kept in the Royal Mews, adjacent to Buckingham Palace.

There has been a Royal Mews in London since the reign of Richard II but in the early days this was a place where the King kept his falcons, birds-of-prey needed for the once popular sport of falconry or hawking. The name 'mews' derives from the Latin 'mutare' — to change, relating to a place of refuge where falcons sheltered while changing their plumage, or 'mewing'. While the original mews were near Charing Cross, the first royal stables were in the suburb of Bloomsbury — known until the late Tudor period as Lomesbury. When the stables in Lomesbury were destroyed in a great fire, during the reign of Henry VIII, the royal stud moved into quarters at Charing Cross, which soon became a centre for horses rather than for birds-of-prey. Although rebuilt by Edward VI and greatly

Left *The Royal Mews.*

Right *The Coronation or State Coach — with box and hammer cloth.*

Below right *The Gold State Coach passing Buckingham Palace* (The Field).

improved by Mary I, the building appears to have been neglected during the 17th century and allowed to fall into decay. New stables or mews were built by George II, in 1732, to the designs of William Kent, an architect and painter also renowned as the 'Father of English Gardening.'

In the third year of his reign George III acquired Buckingham House from Sir Charles Sheffield, formerly the town residence of the Dukes of Buckingham, which he rebuilt as Buckingham Palace. The mews at Charing Cross were still used until the early 19th century, but eventually sharing its functions with stables at Buckingham Palace. In 1825, during the reign of George IV, the complete stables were redesigned and enlarged by John Nash, its date recorded on a weather vane above the front entrance.

The present Royal Mews is a stately and elegant building in the neo-Doric style, mainly surrounding a large courtyard or quadrangle entered from the Buckingham Palace Road. Parts open to the public may be visited on Wednesday and Thursday afternoons, between 2 pm and 4 pm*, except when horses and vehicles are needed for state functions, concerning which announcements are made in the press. The east side of the quadrangle has coach and carriage houses containing most of the vehicles used in public ceremonial which can be viewed at close quarters. In other rooms, mainly on the opposite side of the buildings, are

* Dates and times of opening given here and elsewhere are correct at the time of writing, but readers are advised to check before paying a visit.

displays of saddlery and harness, some items being gifts from distinguished foreign visitors. Perhaps the most outstanding exhibit is the Gold State Coach of England, designed for the wedding of George III and used at every coronation since the reign of George IV. This is a glittering object drawn by eight horses in pairs, each near-side horse ridden by a postilion who drives its fellow, assisted by walking grooms. The coach, weighing upwards of 4 tons, is perhaps too heavy and precious to move at more than walking pace, although formerly driven perhaps slightly faster, from a high box seat. The box and ornate hammer cloth were removed in 1902, during the reign of Edward VII who complained that they obscured his vision and made the interior so dark that he could not be seen by the crowds. The whole point of a public appearance is to see and be seen, yet despite this worthy aim, removing the box has partly destroyed the balance and symmetry of the coach, which would not have been within the aims of either its first

Left *The Royal Mews.*
Above *Funeral horse, late 19th century.*

royal patron or the army of craftsmen labouring to make it the most glamorous state coach in Europe. Electric lighting was eventually installed, worked by concealed batteries.

Carriage and coach horses are stabled to the north west of the quadrangle, kept in stalls on either side of a central gangway. There are four or five loose boxes, added in comparatively recent years, which may be thought better for sick or injured horses. The ceiling is high and the atmosphere spacious, although perhaps seen at its most dramatic in winter with artificial lighting. The Mews' stables have been described as some of the finest in the world, brought up-to-date, but not greatly changed, by Edward VII. They were perhaps matched, or even surpassed, by the stables of the Prince Regent at Brighton, designed by William Porden, but these are no longer used for stabling purposes.

Horses at the Royal Mews appear both alert and contented, a sure sign of fair treatment and the consideration of reserved yet well-mannered staff, some of whom are always on duty in shining top hats and dark frock coats. The scent and noise of horses is all pervading while the roar of city traffic dwindles to a distant hum. Half-close the eyes to the modern dress of the visitors and one could be transported back at least a century in time and mood.

Fashions in horses for ceremonial have changed throughout the years. During the 18th century they were mainly Hanoverian Creams, imported from one of two studs in Germany, by order of George I. It is said they came to be disliked, especially during the First World War, on account of their German name and origins — although in-breeding may have weakened the strain. Although once popular as drum horses with certain cavalry bands and for performing in the circus ring, very few Creams were evident after the Great War. Like many pale coloured animals they were frequently albinos with pink eyes and pinkish-mauve pigmentation of face and body. Bays and blacks came in during the 1920s but while there are still a number of bays most of the blacks only lasted two or three years. Blacks looked most impressive harnessed to state coaches but may have been associated in the public mind with funerals. It may be noted that, until the mid-1930s most undertakers used black horses, imported from Belgium and Holland, to draw their mourning coaches — known as the 'black brigade'.

At the present time horses are either bays or greys, some of the former being Cleveland Bays from Yorkshire, but a number of animals of similar conformation from Ireland, Holland and Germany. The prejudice against German horses no longer exists and Oldenburghers, noted for strength combined with symmetry and smart action, are particularly suitable. Perhaps the most popular horses in the stud are known as 'Windsor Greys', although they are not of any particular breed, but are set apart mainly by their colour and style. A number of grey carriage horses have always been stabled at Windsor, as this was a popular colour, especially with women and young people, throughout the last century. Professional horsemen tended to dislike greys as they were difficult to clean and groom. The horses at Windsor were not always considered up to the heavier duties of full state ceremonial, but greatly improved during the second decade of the present century. George V and Queen Mary always used 'Windsor Greys' for their drive down the course at Ascot races, a subject celebrated by a series of magnificent paintings, the first of which was commissioned by Queen Mary, from the controversial horse and landscape painter Sir Alfred Munnings PRA. One of these paintings is to be seen in a carriage house at the Royal Mews, not least among the many attractions of this place.

Munnings' painting 'Their Majesties return from Ascot' (Reproduced by permission of Frost and Reed Ltd and the Tate Gallery).

Royal coachman in semi-state livery.

Royal postillion.

Broughman.

'Windsor Greys' were so named because they were first kept at Windsor, and because King George V changed the official name of his family to Windsor during the Great War. Examples of the modern type, as used to draw the Gold State Coach at the coronations of both George VI and Elizabeth II, are mainly of Irish blood, although one of the finest was a gift from the last Czar of all the Russias. With Orlov strains, this horse was noted for his near perfect action. The open or state landau in the painting by Munnings was drawn by four horses of which the high-stepping Russian was the ideal ridden leader. During the 1920s and 30s there were numerous carriages, drawn by both greys and bays, taking members of the Royal Family and their guests to seats in the Royal Enclosure. They travelled not only down the course, as in modern times, but from the castle steps and through Windsor Great Park, making a truly regal display. The number of carriages is now greatly reduced, but the splendid action of the horses and smart appearance of the postilions remains — the latter wearing a special Ascot livery of gold, red and black with peaked jockey caps, white leather breeches and top boots.

There is a special costume or livery for each occasion, just as there are also special vehicles, harness and trimmings. Coachmen driving from the box wear full-state, semi-state, plain or scarlet liveries, the most important of these being full-state and including cocked hat, knee breeches, buckled shoes and a braided frock coat. This may sound over-ornate but was not unusual for many private coachmen in service from the early 18th century to the period before the Great War. Only servants employed by officers of the armed services and the Royal Household, were allowed to wear cockades in their hats.

Apart from the state coaches and carriages, including the smart but ornate Irish State Coach, the Scottish State Coach, the so-called Glass Coach and the state landaus, there are several more utilitarian vehicles. Foremost among these is King Edward VII's town coach, the only survivor of several similar coaches used up to the period of the Second World War. This was restored in 1964 and four of its panels replaced by lights or windows to make it a glass coach. It now conveys ambassadors to Buckingham Palace for the ceremony of presenting their credentials, and also sergeants-at-arms in charge of the Royal Mace — an object so large that it often protrudes through a side window. There are also a number of Broughams, Clarences, wagonettes and brakes, used on less formal occasions. The Brougham, originally claimed to have been designed by Lord Brougham and Vaux, is now thought to have been based on an earlier French design, but was certainly modified to suit the needs of this nobleman and became a light but handy vehicle between a cab and a town coach, drawn by a single horse in shafts. There is room for two passengers facing forwards, the upper-front usually having a square glass panel. The example in the Royal Mews is in regular use taking royal messengers and their despatch boxes to Number 10 Downing Street or Government offices in Whitehall. The Clarence was a larger version of the Brougham, with which the same duties are shared, taking four passengers sitting opposite each other, but drawn by a pair of horses harnessed to pole gear.

At rehearsals for state processions large open vehicles known as breaks or brakes (alternative spellings) are frequently used. These are drawn by a pair of

A wagonette (Science Museum).

horses and have longitudinal seats down either side of the interior, used for taking large numbers of people on an outing or to convey items of luggage or furniture from one royal residence to another, in which case the seats can be removed. The design dates from the 1860s and is said to be an enlarged version of the wagonette, frequently used for training and exercising horses, especially to work as pairs. They are frequently seen entering or leaving the royal parks, where many of the dress rehearsals and regular training sessions take place.

Nearly every type of familiar coach and carriage is to be seen at the Royal Mews and it would take several books to describe each in detail. Many are in daily use, while others are for special occasions and a few are retained as curios and museum-pieces. One example worth mentioning is the charabanc, a French design which was the prototype of the modern charabanc or motor coach, originally used for sporting purposes and to attend race-meetings, having parallel rows of crosswise seating. This particular example was one of the earliest designs of its type and was presented to Queen Victoria by Louis Phillipe, King of the French.

The Royal Mews is a department of the Queen's Household, presided over by the Crown Equerry, usually a former military officer. One of his many tasks is to purchase new horses and select them for their various duties. The first Crown Equerry was a Major Richard Groves appointed in 1854, also known as Secretary to the Master of the Horse and Superintendent of the Royal Mews. Until that date direct control of the Mews and carriages had been exercised by the Master of the Horse, who holds a high office of state next to the Lord Chamberlain and the Lord Steward. The Master of the Horse ceased to take an executive interest from about

1859, after which date his area of control was renamed the Royal Mews Department. Yet even today he is the third greatest officer at the court, in attendance on the Royal Family whenever horses are involved for ceremonial purposes. One of the most popular Masters of the Horse was the 10th Duke of Beaufort, appointed in 1936 during the short reign of Edward VIII, but holding this post until 1978. A former Household Cavalryman he served under four sovereigns. The present Master, also commissioned in the Blues and Royals, is the Earl of Westmorland whose ancestor was Master of the Horse to George III from 1795 to 1798.

Both state occasions and their rehearsals need time consuming effort. The Mews are always busy, especially the farrier's shop, each horse being reshod at least once a month with studded shoes to prevent slipping on frozen or greasy roads. Harness of all types is kept in a high state of polish and repair, ready for immediate use. Everything is cleaned and refurbished at the end of each drive, however long this may take. A yard at the back of the main quadrangle, rarely seen by the public, is known as the carriage wash, where some of the Broughams and brakes are normally kept. All vehicles returning from road work are wheeled straight into this area, washed and polished to the smallest detail. Rain or shine, there is at least 1½ hours harness exercise each day, mainly on busy roads with Brougham, brake or wagonette. When the weather is too severe there is work round the sheltered quadrangle or in a covered riding school, often accompanied by waving flags and crowd noises, supplied by anyone handy for the purpose. This makes excellent training for the excitement of a big occasion.

On the actual day of ceremonial there is always a feeling of supressed excitement. The complex harness is laid-out on wooden framed saddle-horses of polished mahogany. With the full state kit there are many decorations, streamers and giant rosettes, these latter having to be laced into the mane and along the neck ridge of each horse. Everyone is pressed into service and even apprentices are thrown in at the deep end, trying hard to follow instructions and not look as confused as they must often feel. Horses are shampooed and groomed with the maximum elbow grease, then led into the courtyard for putting to in traces or shafts. Coachmen and postilions are not allowed to help at this stage to prevent soiling their spotless gloves and liveries. With the teams in position hoofs may be given a final oiling and polish, after which there is a close inspection of every detail, especially traces. An order is given 'Stand at the Ready', which is the signal to prepare to mount. Encumbered by whips and leg guards, each rider has to be given a leg-up and almost lifted onto the high, old-fashioned saddles. Having taken the reins the coachmen mount their box seats and the procession moves off, going round to what they still call the 'front of the house' to collect the family.

Civic coaches

At one time many of the larger and more important cities had their fleets of coaches and carriages to be used on ceremonial occasions. The City of London has the Lord Mayor's Coach, almost as famous as, but a few years older than, the Gold State Coach. In former days the Lord Mayor rode through the streets on his own horse but city merchants like John Gilpin, although they might drill the trained bands to perfection and speak eloquence at banquets, often proved third rate horsemen. After one Lord Mayor elect was thrown from his horse and seriously injured, it was decided to build an elaborate but comfortable coach from City funds. This was designed by Joseph Berry, a master coach-builder and senior partner in the firm of Berry and Barker, and completed in 1757. It was a lumbering affair of gilt and red paintwork, with a bright red hammer cloth. The door panels were attributed to the Florentine artist Ciprianni, who also painted the Royal State Coach. The present coach owned by the City of London, however, is not the original but an exact replica, built in 1896 and weighing 3 tons 16 cwts.

On the second Saturday in November the new Lord Mayor drives to the Law Courts where his is sworn in and signs his declaration of office, returning to the Mansion House in full state. He heads a procession of carriages and cars, containing Aldermen and other dignitaries who act as his witnesses, while there are marching bands, units of the armed forces and colourful floats representing crafts, trades and industries. This is known collectively as 'The Lord Mayor's Show' and expected to represent a different theme each year. Many of the horses and vehicles are hired from jobbers or contractors, while the six heavy horses drawing the coach itself are owned by the firm of Whitbreads, who now take responsibility for its upkeep and maintenance, also providing a coachman, grooms and a postilion for the near-side leader, from their staff. At the side of the coach march pikemen of the Honourable Artillery Company, wearing 17th century half armour and plumed helmets, representing one of the oldest volunteer units in the British Army. When not in use the vehicle is kept in a humidified

The State Coach of The Lord Mayor of London (Whitbreads).

The Speaker's Coach.

chamber that prevents the woodwork from cracking and warping. The high box-seat has to be mounted by means of a step-ladder. It may be viewed at the London Museum.

Whitbreads are now also responsible for the upkeep of the Speaker's Coach, used by the Speaker of the House of Commons, which appears less frequently than the Lord Mayor's Coach. It was last used in public on 7th June 1977, taking part in the Silver Jubilee celebrations of Elizabeth II. It is driven from the box to a pair of grey Shires, further attended by two men in tail coats and jockey caps, known as running footmen. At the Silver Jubilee the coachman was Charlie Ruocco, normally the foreman horsekeeper at Whitbread's Chiswell Street Stables, who served as running footman at the Coronation, twenty-five years earlier. For many years the Speaker's Coach was housed at the Royal Mews but in 1977 it was handed over to Whitbreads, by whom it is now stored at Chiswell Street under special protection.

There have been several interesting connections between Whitbreads and the Speaker's Coach, throughout its long history. Charles Lefevre, later Lord Eversley, a partner in the family firm, married a daughter of Samuel Whitbread and later became Speaker of the House of Commons, from 1839 to 1857. The brewery has frequently horsed the vehicle, memorable occasions being events leading to the Diamond Jubilee of Queen Victoria, the Silver Jubilee of George V and the Coronations of Edward VII, George V, George VI and Elizabeth II. It dates from the late Stuart period and was designed by Daniel Marot for William III. Queen Anne gave the coach to the Speaker of her day to be used exclusively by him and his successors. It weighs nearly three tons and is suspended, like the Gold State Coach and the Lord Mayor's Coach, on thoroughbraces or lengthwise straps of toughened leather attached to iron pillars.

Another state coach of great elegance and refinement is owned by the Corporation of Dublin, recently restored by skilled craftsmen working for the authority. It was originally drawn by six horses but is now hauled by a team of four, all of which are loaned as required by the Guinness family. Although planned as early as the 1760s and intended to rival, if not surpass the state coach of the Lord Mayor of London, with whom there was friendly rivalry, it did not appear for nearly thirty years. Its first official journey was made in 1791, the team wearing red morocco harness, trimmed with green and silver. Black harness was introduced in 1808, a modified version of which is still used. Although an original budget limit had been set at £400 the total cost was nearer £3,000, which reflects the dramatic increase in costs and current inflation towards the end of the century. Unlike the Lord Mayor's Coach this vehicle may be drawn at a dignified trot, using much lighter horses. For most of the time it is on show to the public, as a museum-piece, along with its elaborate harness and the liveries of coachmen, grooms, and footmen. When drawn by six horses the leading pair were controlled by a postilion in jockey cap and shell jacket, although the coachman wears the once familiar tricorn hat with tail-coat and plush knee breeches.

Bristol is one of the few remaining provincial cities providing coaches and horses for its civic dignitaries. These are under the care of the Transport Department of Bristol City Council. Both horses and vehicles are kept at stables adjacent to Ashton Court on the outskirts of the City, formerly the home of the Smythe family, where Edward VII was a frequent guest.

There are now three vehicles in regular use, these being a high-perched semi-state coach (slightly smaller than an ordinary state coach), a semi-state landau and an open vehicle known as the 'Proclamation Brake' — from which the City Clerk reads Royal Proclamations and other important announcements. When the semi-state coach is used it is normally preceded by the City Sword-bearer and escorted by mounted policemen. Horses are usually chestnut geldings of Irish origins, although in past years both Dutch and German horses have been used. Irish horses are preferred both for their reliable temperament and firm bone structure. They are undeterred by the heaviest traffic and able to cope with many steep gradients in and around the city area. All vehicles were made by the master coach builder Fuller of Bristol, during the middle of the last century, and are kept in exceptionally good condition. Fully aware of the hazards to older vehicles in modern traffic, the emphasis is on safety and a high standard of maintenance.

Stable routine at Ashton Court begins at 7 am with the first feed of the day, followed by mucking-out, grooming and a general check on harness and vehicles. During the course of the morning there is $1\frac{1}{2}$ hours road work and exercise in full harness. Afternoons are spent in cleaning harness, vehicles and other equipment. There are four feeds per day, with a bran mash at weekends.

Although a large number of people both local and visitors enjoy seeing the 'coaches' as they are termed, there have been criticisms from those who feel the expenditure involved is both unnecessary and inappropriate. It is defended as a tradition that should be kept alive and cherished as part of our common heritage — once allowed to lapse this would be difficult, almost impossible to regain, leaving the city much poorer in spiritual and aesthetic values.

At the time of writing Liverpool has recently disposed of its civic coach and horses, although the City of Hereford has undertaken the restoration of its pre-1850 dress Clarence, for occasional use, drawn by a matching pair. Work in this department was undertaken by J. D. M. Abercrombie of Gloucester, who also produces large numbers of vehicles in connection with a 'Driving for the Disabled Scheme', sponsored by the British Driving Society.

Ceremonial coaches overseas

At the Windsor Horse Show of 1978 the British public was privileged to see a selection of vehicles and horses from the Dutch Royal Mews at the Hague. These paraded in the main show ring by kind permission of the Queen of the Netherlands and were drawn by smart teams of Gelderlanders. The earliest and most attractive was a glass coach of the 1820s, its roof surmounted by a replica of the Royal Crown of Orange. It was designed for King William I as a state coach but, in later years, was reserved mainly for royal weddings. An elegant cream-coloured barouche of French design, drawn by a team of six, in the care of postilions, it was without a box and greatly admired for lightness and grace.

Details concerning the State Carriage of Canada, now in the care of the Royal Canadian Mounted Police, are discussed in a further chapter. This is drawn by a team of six black horses and normally kept at RCMP headquarters in Ottawa.

Chapter 2

Army horses

The horse in warfare

Horses have been used in warfare since the dawn of history, a fact no less deplorable to many animal lovers than war itself. During the late 1930s the British cavalry was almost entirely mechanised, greeted by many as a sign that horses would no longer appear amidst the horror and carnage of modern battlefields. Yet such rejoicing may have been premature as while the British Army was casting large numbers of its troop horses — officers retaining their chargers for cere-monial purposes — the Germans and other foreign armies were still buying them in large numbers. Despite the urge to mechanise in all departments of life, both civil and military, certain lessons had been taught (if not always learnt or understood) in the Spanish Civil War, Abyssinia and even during periods of unrest in our own colonial empire. It may be noted that the staunchest resistance in warfare is made in the most difficult country such as mountains, jungle and deeply wooded areas which form natural lines of defence. These were parts where

Royal Army Service Corps pack horses are watered on a march (Royal Corps of Transport Museum, Aldershot).

Make much of your horses.

tanks and lorries (as then developed) were, if not useless, almost as much a liability as an asset. While a wrecked or broken horse wagon was soon pushed off the road a few badly damaged tanks and other mechanical vehicles could delay the advance or retreat of an army in the most serious manner, hampering mobility on forest tracks and in mountain passes, out of all proportion to their successful use on the open plain, where they were even better targets for dive bombers than unmechanised troops.

From the view point of economics and logistics the Germans maintained that horse transport in the rear, even supporting swiftly moving panzer divisions, represented a worthwhile saving in money, fuel and man-power. Throughout the Second World War, especially on the Eastern Front, great use was still made of horsed units, not always in battle but to drag guns, field cookers and supply carts. It may astonish many to learn that more horses and mules were killed during the Second World War, despite mechanisation of the British armed forces, than during the First when the tank was in its infancy and general service wagons, each

Left *Swedish war cart c1940.*

Right *The Warwickshire Yeomanry advancing in Syria during World War 2. From a painting by Major W.P. Moss* (Imperial War Museum).

drawn by a pair of horses, greatly outnumbered motor lorries and traction engines.

It is now clear that Britain and France lost the initiative in Norway, during the early part of the Second World War, through not having sufficient pack horses for winter warfare in mountainous terrain. Attempts were being made, at training centres in the Scottish Highlands, to prepare and assemble such units at the time when Norway finally capitulated and Allied troops were forced to withdraw. Needless to say the German invaders had embarked with large numbers of horses and pack ponies, belonging to their mountain warfare units. These remained active throughout the conflict, especially in Greece, Crete and the Balkans.

While this may not be the place for extensive military theorising it should be recorded that the reconquest of Burma, Southern Italy and Abysinnia would have been impossible without large numbers of horses, camels, mules and even asses. Mounted regiments of the British regular cavalry, supported by yeomanry or territorial cavalry, the Arab Legion, Free French and Polish units, made considerable impact throughout the Middle East, although mainly in a defensive role, during the early part of the war. It should be remembered that in 1939 Palestine occupied a vital key position but was involved in a deadly civil war during which it was essential that railways, pipelines and frontiers were kept under surveillance, for which mounted patrols were ideal.

Several countries such as India, China and republics in South America still keep regular mounted units to guard and patrol their less accessible frontiers, while even in Europe a few NATO countries partly rely on pack horses and mules to defend their territory in Alpine passes or snow-girt forests. Both Norway and Sweden have units of rangers which keep stocky mountain ponies for pack work or pulling sledges, although these are used more to supplement than replace motorised vehicles on tracks or runners. Mechanical faults are far from unlikely, however, in sub-zero temperatures and neither routine patrols nor full-scale manoeuvres can be postponed by such disasters. It may be noted that the

Norwegian Army has about a thousand horses and ponies distributed throughout the country, many hired to civilian farmers and foresters but recalled to active service in times of national emergency.

While the days of conventional glamour, with brazen trumpets and tossing plumes, has long disappeared from the scene of action, to be replaced by dismounted horse-leaders or a species of mounted infantry, certain troops are also trained for ceremonial duties, escorting processions and forming honour guards. Cavalry used in this context also frequently double as mounted police, while retaining a nucleus of men trained in horsemanship and the care of horses for unforseen emergencies. It is a wise policy to retain as many options as possible and those who denigrate the efficiency of animals in modern warfare should remember their use by the Household Cavalry in troubled Cyprus, during the 1960s, when patrols were sent out on donkeys and mules through areas in which tanks would have been far too conspicuous. Although horses were not used during actual fighting in the Falkland Islands, they have since been employed for patrol work in an experimental context, also as pack animals to supply lonely outposts with food and ammunition. It is claimed that many of the animals used are descendents of Welsh Cobs and ponies taken to the Falklands by British settlers over fifty years ago.

Most of the animals were rounded-up and retrained under the supervision of Sergeant Graham Carter of the Royal Army Veterinary Corps, to whom the author was introduced while a guest of the Corps at their headquarters in Melton Mowbray, Leicestershire, early in 1984. Up to that time horses and ponies were mainly used to supply strongpoints in a mountainous area near San Carlos Bay, their pack saddles creaking under water containers, food packs, spare parts and even missiles. The cost of sending a helicopter on these deliveries worked out at £8,000 per hour, making nonsense of an earlier decision to abandon pack units of the Royal Corps of Transport, working under similar conditions in the Hong Kong New Territories.

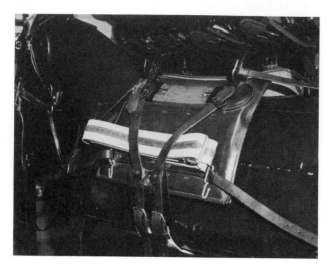

Left *Pack harness as used in the Falkland Islands, 1984* (RAVC Depot, Melton Mowbray – T. Edgson).

Below right *Officer of the Blues and Royals.*

Below far right *Drum horse of the Life Guards.*

The Household Cavalry

There are at present four regular mounted units in the British Army. Perhaps the most glamourous to the average layman is the mounted regiment of the Household Cavalry. This is a combined unit drawing recruits from both the Life Guards and the Blues and Royals. From the late 18th century the Life Guards were mustered as two regiments, members of the second regiment traditionally drawn from Scotland.

The first regiment of Life Guards was founded in 1660 at the Restoration of Charles II, mainly from cavaliers who followed him into exile after the Civil Wars. They were the senior regiment in the newly formed standing army of that period, later joined by two regiments of foot guards and the Royal Horse Guards or Blues. The Horse Guards, as a military unit, were even older than the Life Guards, although not so close to the King's person, having previously served under Cromwell and General Monck. Although the Horse Guards were originally known as Upton Crook's Regiment, their first royalist commanding officer was the Earl of Oxford. Like most colonels in those days he was responsible for the well-being of his men and for the choice of their uniform. He clothed his new command in dark blue tunics, earning them their first nickname of 'Oxford Blues', later shortened to 'Blues'. Although frequently brigaded with the Life Guards, they did not become official members of the Household Cavalry until 1820 when their Colonel, the Duke of Wellington, was granted the title of 'Silver-Stick-in-Waiting', being close to the King's person as an inner bodyguard, an appointment shared with 'Gold-Stick-in-Waiting' of the Life Guards.

The Second Life Guards were raised in 1788. As with the First Life Guards they wore red tunics and white plumes, the latter made not from real feathers but finely shredded whalebone. The two regiments were amalgamated to become 'The Life Guards' as the result of defence economies in 1922, which led to the disbanding or integration of many fine regiments. From 1941 the Household Cavalry was transformed into two armoured regiments, grouped — for tactical purposes — with the Royal Armoured Corps, which had absorbed most of the line cavalry five years earlier. They were still regarded as cavalry and in later years it was their concern to provide one mechanised regiment each, either at Windsor or abroad, and one horsed squadron each for London duties. For many years the horse and foot guards were known collectively as the Household Brigade or the Brigade of Guards, although the term correctly belonged to the five regiments of footguards forming an infantry brigade. Cavalry and infantry should be in separate brigades, although able to combine as a division. In 1951, to avoid further confusion, George VI decreed that his household troops should be known as the Household Division or Guards Division. For this reason all recruits to the Life Guards and Horse Guards were sent for basic training to the depot of the foot guards at Pirbright in Surrey. Under an army reduction plan of 1969 the Horse Guards were amalgamated with the 1st Royal Dragoons, the senior cavalry regiment of the line also raised during the reign of Charles II, to become the 'Blues and Royals'.

Combined squadrons from both Life Guards and Blues and Royals are now known as the 'Mounted Regiment', but retain clearly marked identities. Each horsed squadron provides six commissioned officers and a hundred and eleven

other ranks. Each has its own mounted band of highly trained instrumentalists. Trumpeters always ride greys, while there are four skewbalds for drum horses, two for each regiment — one each being in reserve or under training. This helps to make a total of 240 troop horses and chargers of which 215 are black for general duty purposes. Other horses stabled with the mounted regiment, at Knightsbridge Barracks, include several ceremonial chargers ridden by officers of the foot guards, above the rank of Captain.

Household Cavalry recruits are accepted between the ages of 18 and 25, although some join an affiliated regiment of junior leaders, at the age of 16 or straight from school. Basic training, as previously mentioned, is now concentrated at Pirbright, where many instructors are from the foot guards. For sixteen weeks there is nothing but foot drill, PT and weapons training. The recruit may not touch or see a horse but is asked to commit himself either to the Life Guards or the Blues and Royals from his day of enlistment. After passing out from Pirbright the young troopers are sent to Knightsbridge, where they commence a twenty week course in riding and the care of horses, including basic cavalry training. Part of the course is also conducted at Combermere Barracks, Windsor, with cross country riding in Windsor Great Park. By the end of five and a half months they are qualified to take part in full-dress parades and ceremonial drill.

It is now considered that few young men entering the cavalry have much experience of horses. They learn to ride from scratch also how to groom, feed and generally care for their mounts to whom they soon become greatly attached. For the first week, only half an hour a day is spent in the saddle. This is increased to upwards of three hours, often in full kit, during the final weeks of the course. The recruit eventually graduates to become a trained soldier and dutyman, with his place in a troop. He may also seek further instruction in a number of trades from trumpeter to farrier, saddler and remount rider — the latter training and exercising young horses. The best horsemen may become riding instructors and spend the greater part of their military careers teaching others to ride. The majority, not specialist tradesmen, spend three or four years in mounted duties, according to rank, then transfer to the armoured squadrons for overseas-operational service.

Life at Knightsbridge can be highly demanding for both men and horses but at least there is now a background of modest comfort, in contrast to the earlier or Victorian barracks. The older building, although more picturesque, was draughty, dark and over-crowded with twenty men sharing a small room. There are now only four men to a comparatively spacious room, with facilities for storing both kit and personal belongings. Gone are the folding iron beds and straw-filled mattresses, with a tiny locker and shelf above each bed. The new barracks were designed by Sir Basil Spence, also the architect of the modern Coventry Cathedral, and were opened in 1970. Stabling is in a two-tiered block overlooking Hyde Park, having under floor heating, an automatic watering system and electric grooming equipment. In former times water was not available for the horses in their stalls and each morning there was a queue at the outside water troughs, known as watering order, the men shivering in slacks and shirt sleeves. In

Farrier Corporal Major of the Household Cavalry.

present day idiom long training rides are known as watering order, reminiscent of the constant search for fresh water while on campaign in foreign parts.

A typical day in the mounted regiment starts at 6 am, with reveille sounded by one of the squadron (duty) trumpeters, although on days of state ceremonial preparations might begin two hours earlier. Grooming and cleaning begins about twenty minutes later while officers appear on the scene, after a special call, at ten minutes past seven. Daily duties involve guard mounting at Whitehall, escorts for visiting dignitaries and rehearsals for ceremonial parades and processions.

After grooming and saddling-up the men ride on to the parade ground. Here the two Squadron Leaders, shadowed by their trumpeters, fall-in at the heads of their respective commands. The ranks are soon ordered to attention and the Commanding Officer makes his appearance, followed by the sounding of the Royal Salute. The Standard arrives and is then handed, with due ceremony, to the Standard-bearer and his mounted escort.

By 7:15 am the guards move off to their duties, many to attend rehearsals and practice rides, either in the park or through London streets and squares. They are preceded in true cavalry fashion, by scouts or points, while the rearguard is covered by a further detached unit. Trumpeters make signals for certain movements while a large body of men and horses are always accompanied by the regimental farriers, wearing dark plumes and carrying ceremonial pole-axes, with which they formerly destroyed horses too seriously wounded or injured to recover. Some laymen mistake these pole-axes for medieval-type battle axes, while others

Above left *The Life Guards leaving Hyde Park, 1982* (Ministry of Defence).

Above right *The saddlery of a British Cavalryman* (RAVC Depot, Melton Mowbray – T. Edgson).

suspect that at least one of them is the infamous headsman's axe from the Tower of London! All movements on parade are closely watched by the riding instructors, known to young soldiers as the dreaded 'blue mafia'.

At some stage or other of their practice rides the troopers are waylaid by organised groups of rowdies, waving hats, blowing whistles and making a general hub-bub. This is done, as at the Royal Mews, to ensure that horses are well-behaved and keep their dressing even in the most testing circumstances. A few horses slip down on metalled roads, despite wearing studs for a better grip, while some occasionally collide with motor vehicles. A taxi or saloon car driven at the normal speed usually comes off second best but there have been a few cases of severe injuries to both horse and man. Ray Milland, the celebrated film actor who formerly served in the Royal Horse Guards, recorded in his autobiography how his horse bolted in the Mall, while on escort duty. He returned to Buckingham Palace well in advance of the rest of the procession, having scraped-off a few inches of skin on the metal hub cap or naff end of a carriage wheel. In such a plight the unfortunate trooper must return to barracks alone and await a searching inquest. A man who is thrown by his horse and still able to walk, is expected to go in search of his mount almost before he has time to dust himself down. As may be imagined, playing cowboys in Hyde Park or a busy London street, especially encumbered by sword, cloak and long boots, is a far from amusing way to spend the morning.

The daily guard mounting ceremony is perhaps one of the highlights of London duty, and a must for all foreign tourists. This takes place in a courtyard of the guard house at Whitehall, one of the few remaining parts of this former royal palace to survive a great fire. The gateway through the guard house leading on to the Horse Guards Parade may be termed the entrance to 'Royal London'. Beyond it lie the royal parks, palaces and barracks of the Household troops. Unauthorised wheeled traffic, both cars and carriages, are not allowed to drive through the archway and are turned back by sentries if the occupants are unable to show the 'ivories' or official passes. The latter are only fifty in number, distributed to certain ambassadors, High Commissioners and members of the Royal Household. In the days of universal horse tansport when a passage through archway and courtyard represented a time saving short-cut, the ivories were greatly in demand. They also represented a status symbol.

The Queen's Lifeguard to occupy the gatehouse is now chosen, on alternate days, from the Life Guards or the Blues and Royals. It is either a long guard or a short guard according to whether or not the soverign resides in London. If the Royal Standard is flying over Buckingham Palace the long guard sets out from Knightsbridge commanded by a Captain or Subaltern. The short guard is a

Future drum horse of the Household Cavalry (RAVC Depot, Melton Mowbray).

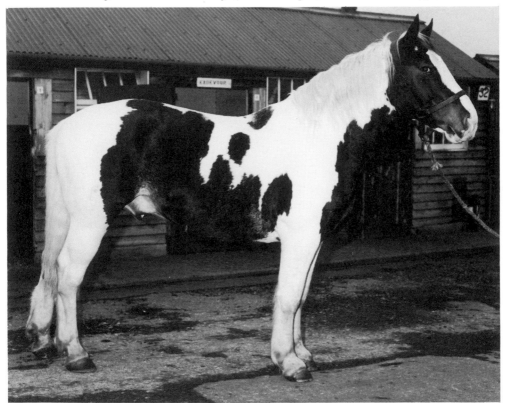

smaller body of men under the command of a Corporal of Horse (a Sergeant in the Household Cavalry). Guard mounting duties continued throughout the Great War by men wounded at the front and no longer fit for overseas service. There was a guard in service dress, with rifles instead of swords, during the first part of the Second World War, when a Household Cavalry Training Regiment was stationed in London and Windsor — mainly drawn from reservists and recruits, although in later years this was abandoned and the large sentry boxes used as air raid shelters. In all cases four sentry posts have to be filled, there being mounted sentries or boxmen spending one hour on and one hour off, while dismounted men spend longer periods patrolling archway and courtyard. It is the dismounted soldier who makes the first challenge, calling on the boxmen only when in difficulties. Boxmen, elegant in polished cuirass or breastplate are the stars of the show and frequently photographed on their impassive horses. Some tourists and well-wishers are known to sidle-up to the mounted sentries and slip gifts of money, sweetmeats and cigarettes inside their jack-boots. These are not always appreciated as hard objects are uncomfortable in warm weather while sweets soon melt into a sticky mess. There is, however, great competition to be picked as boxman and those chosen for the honour, depending on their smartness of turn-out and the grooming of their horses, are eligible for the Princess Elizabeth silver cup, awarded at Windsor Horse Show during the spring of each year.

At the end of the London season the Household Cavalry mounted squadrons spend a fortnight under canvas at Stoney Castle in Surrey. In former days they rode from the centre of London to their camp site but caused such dislocation of

The Mounted Regiment of the Household Cavalry practise the 'Charge' for a tattoo in Rushmoor Arena, Aldershot, 1970 (Daily Telegraph).

traffic that it was later decided to send the horses in boxes, while the men followed in coaches and lorries. The fourteen day camp is greatly enjoyed by both men and horses, especially if the weather is fine. There are map reading exercises and show-jumping or cross country riding events, but all in a far less formal atmosphere than at Knightsbridge, Windsor or Whitehall. At the end of the summer camp they begin training for the first great event on their calender, which is the State Opening of Parliament in November. This is only equalled in importance, as a regular event, by the Trooping of the Colour.

The Household Cavalry are also renowned for their musical rides, to be seen at horse shows and military tattoos throughout the country. Perhaps the best-known of these, less frequently seen in later years, is a full-dress affair with gleaming helmets and breastplates, each trooper carrying a tall lance with fluttering pennon. Compared with the hell for leather drive of the King's Troop, it is a slow and stately affair. Far more exciting is the activity ride and mounted quadrille with soldiers wearing pillbox caps and the undress or less formal uniform of the 1880s, which has featured at the Royal Tournament and several international horse shows from the late Victorian era to the present day.

The King's Troop, Royal Horse Artillery

For many years the Royal Artillery, the largest corps in the British Army, was divided into three sections, known as Horse Artillery, Field Artillery and Garrison Artillery. While the Garrison Artillery were responsible for howitzers and siege guns, the Field Artillery supported the infantry and the Horse Artillery, known as the 'galloping gunners', supported the swifter moving cavalry. When the majority of line cavalry regiments were absorbed into the Royal Armoured Corps the Horse Artillery retrained to use light tractors and smaller guns mounted on pneumatic tyres, keeping up with tanks and armoured cars of other mechanised units. The remnant of horse gunners, mainly responsible for training artillerymen in the skills of horesmanship, once necessary in all brances of the corps, was known as the 'Riding House Troop' stationed, at the outbreak of the Second World War, in St John's Wood Barracks, North West London.

It had been a peace-time tradition that a battery of guns from the 'Wood' should fire salutes in Hyde Park on royal birthdays, to welcome foreign visitors to this country and at the State Opening of Parliament. The last battery to perform these duties before the outbreak of hostilities was also one of the few remaining mounted units in the British Army. In keeping alive a proud tradition they were of great interest to King George VI who, when releasing them for overseas duties, wished it to be known that either this or a similar battery should return to London for ceremonial duties, as soon as the war was over. In 1945 the King sent a personal message to the 'Wood' asking that a salute, with mounted gunners, should be fired on his next birthday. The Riding House Troop, now returned to their former headquarters, were quick to respond and a saluting battery brought into being, using 13 pounder guns and their limbers that had been kept in storage over a period of five years. Such keenness was shown by officers and men involved that the King made a visit of inspection and graciously offered to sign the visitor's

Royal Horse Artillery c1815.

book. Yet above his signature at the head of the page, he struck out the word 'Riding' and substituted 'King's Troop'. When Queen Elizabeth II came to the throne she decreed that 'King's Troop' should remain the official title of the saluting battery, in memory of her deceased father and his interest in their work.

While retaining and refurbishing skills required in mounted gunnery, the functions of the King's Troop are almost entirely ceremonial. Apart from saluting duties in Hyde Park, having the traditional right to pass through rather than round the gateway of Marble Arch, the troop appears at the Lord Mayor's Show and in other state processions, and provides a gun carriage and team of black horses for state funerals. The Kings and Queens of England, Sir Winston Churchill and Field Marshal Montgomery all passed to their last resting place drawn by six blacks of the Royal Horse Artillery.

Perhaps the most spectacular and unique contribution to military pageantry made by the Troop is its musical drive, featured each year at the Royal Tournament and at many horse or agricultural shows throughout Britain and abroad. The weaving in-and-out of guns and limbers to the sound of lively music is a spectacle unequalled in the modern world.

The King's Troop now has an establishment of two hundred horses at St John's Wood, but is a smaller and perhaps more intimate unit than the Household Cavalry at Kightsbridge. While the typical Life Guard, Horse Guard or dragoon has always been a tall man on a big horse, typical of the heavy cavalry, the horse artilleryman seems lighter and more active in the style of a hussar. His horse tends to be a smaller but better quality animal, full of energy but responsive to the slightest touch or aid. It has been said that the general feeling or atmosphere of the Troop is relaxed, although well-disciplined, but not having to rely so much on the influence of the Drill-Sergeant and wearisome clamour of the barrack square. There are few cross-postings and members of the Troop frequently stay in the same unit for the whole of their military careers.

The King's Troop, Royal Horse Artillery c1980.

Although spending most of his service life with horses and in stables a member of the King's Troop is also an artilleryman and spends the first few weeks of his training at Woolwich, the main Artillery Depot. Before making up his mind as to a future role, he is invited to spend a day or two at St John's Wood, where he is shown round and initiated into both the rewards and penalties of working with horses. He must accept the challenges of life at the Wood and be accepted in return, prepared to work as part of a fully constructive team.

After twelve weeks at Woolwich, having decided to join the Troop, the average recruit spends a further three weeks in training with horses, then, after a brief interval, joins a more advanced equitation course to become a detachment rider. The latter are men with drawn sabres, riding at the rear of the guns, who dismount to fire them, while the horse teams retire a short distance to clear for action. It is the drivers rather than the riders who are the stars of the Troop. Each of the six horse gun teams has three drivers, riding and driving a pair between them, like postilions. To make a successful and fully responsible lead driver, riding the near-side leader, takes at least four to five years hard training. Those wishing to embark on this course must prove their dedication as horsemen and commence as centre-driver, rising to rear-driver and eventually to lead-driver. Performing complex evolutions at full stretch, often in a small area is no easy task, needing courage, concentration and the judgement of a good eye. The 13-pounders were of a type introduced during the 1900s, last used in warfare as late as 1941. Gun and limber or ammunition cart form an articulated unit weighing $1\frac{1}{2}$ tons of solid steel and wood. They may travel at the gallop between fifteen and twenty miles per hour, but there are no brakes or springs and each item may be termed a dead weight. The only means by which the guns are controlled is through the nimble feet of the horses, the aids of the drivers and the strength of the traces. Practice drives are usually held not at St John's Wood but in fields reserved for the purpose at Wormwood Scrubs.

Above *The King's Troop of the Royal Horse Artillery at St John's Wood, 1972* (Daily Telegraph).

Left *Breast collar as used in gun teams of the Royal Horse Artillery* (RAVC Depot, Melton Mowbray).

Above right *Horse ambulance at 'The Horse of the Year Show' forming part of a display of early military transport provided by the King's Troop, RHA* (Museum of Military Transport).

The facilities at St John's Wood are as modern as those at Knightsbridge. The greater part of the old barracks was rebuilt during the early 1970s and reoccupied by the King's Troop in 1972. For two and a half years the horse gunners shared quarters with the Household Cavalry at Windsor, just as the Life Guards and Blues shared Wellington Barracks with the foot guards, during a rebuilding stint in Hyde Park. The new barracks have fitted-wardrobes and cupboards, streamlined ablutions, drying and pressing rooms and stabling that is both light and spacious. The only large building left unchanged is the riding school, originally built as a cavalry training centre and indoor ride, being considered a gem of early 19th century architecture. The inner dimensions of the building are 134 ft by 60 ft.

As with the Household Cavalry, a trained soldier may qualify for a number of skilled trades, ranging from farrier and saddler to trumpeter and transport driver. Numbers of assistants are needed in all departments and those not able to make the grade as a detachment rider or driver frequently serve in a general capacity, known as limber gunners.

The King's Troop always spends two weeks of the late summer under canvas, but unlike the Household Cavalry is not limited to a particular venue. They are free to pitch their tents in any part of mainland Britain but prefer a fairly open tract with plenty of room for cross-country riding. There are many opportunities for men serving in the King's Troop to take part in equestrian sports and pastimes, perhaps even more than in other mounted units. These may include show jumping and eventing, organised by either military or civilian authorities, point-to-pointing and riding to hounds. An impressive number of stars, both in show jumping and horse trials, have emerged from the Troop, including at least one Olympic medalist.

Regular salutes are now fired in Hyde Park to celebrate the actual birthday of the Queen, her official birthday, the birthdays of the Duke of Edinburgh and the Queen Mother, the State Opening of Parliament, the arrival in Britain of guests of the state and anniversaries of the Coronation and the Accession. Each event is marked by the firing of forty one rounds.

The Royal Corps of Military Police

The Royal Corps of Military Police still have an important mounted branch, mainly used in the Aldershot District to guard Ministry of Defence property and control military traffic. There are about 20 horses on the strength, mainly in the

Left *Tent-pegging.*

Right *Mounted Royal Corps of Military Police in a review at their Colchester Headquarters* (Ministry of Defence).

Far right *Corporal Williams RCMP c1920* (M. Williams).

keeping of 160 Provost Company, with perhaps one or two at the Colchester Depot. Mounted units of the Military Police formerly served at all overseas depots and theatres of war where there were other mounted troops, but since the numerical decline of this arm, are now concentrated nearer to base.

In one sense members of the Provost Company, although few in numbers, are the true inheritors of the cavalry traditions of the British Army. Although taking full part in ceremonial parades and mounted sports, their main work is strictly functional and a necessary part of the national defence scheme.

Some of the finest horsemen in the army have belonged to the Royal Corps of Military Police, gaining enviable reputations in mounted skill-at-arms and tent-pegging. They work in close co-operation with motor cycle units, between whom there is friendly rivalry. The mounted men frequently challenge their mechanised comrades to a duel at spearing the ring or tent-pegging, lancers on the motorbikes riding pillion. Honours are equally divided but mounted men often have the advantage on the turn. It may be noted that tent-pegging was first practised in India and akin to the up-market sport of pig-sticking, although having a strictly practical aim, training cavalrymen to collapse enemy tents in a surprise attack.

At many shows and military tournaments the military police give a breath-taking display of self-confidence when sharing the arena with trick-riding motor cyclists. The climax of their act is a thrilling scissor-cross or figure of eight movement in which horsemen and bikers alternate at full-throttle to miss each other by split seconds and fractions of an inch.

Recruits for this branch of the army are not allowed direct entry, but have to be fully experienced in other military policework, before selection. Candidates must be 5 ft 7 in or over in height, and should not have had any serious civil convictions. The horses are also specially trained and selected, chosen for dependability and good temperament. Most of them are said to have Roman or convex noses which is thought to be a sign of good character in a horse, if not always of the highest

breeding. Smaller and lighter than troop horses of the Household Cavalry, they are more akin to ridden and driven horses of the King's Troop, RHA.

Saddlery and equipment used in the Provost Company is much the same as that formerly issued to hussars, lancers and dragoons over a period of forty years up to the era of mechanisation. The bamboo, steel-tipped lances, however, only appear for escort duties and at ceremonial parades. At the Coronation of Queen Elizabeth II, mounted military police provided carriage escorts for the Queen of Tonga and the Sultan of Zanzibar.

Other military horses

Some of these, especially ponies, may be used as regimental mascots, while others are ceremonial chargers for officers of the foot guards.

A few formerly mounted regiments, such as the 3rd Queen's Own Hussars, still retain drum horses, which appear at all regimental inspections and full-dress parades. The Drum Sergeant of the Queen's Own Hussars wears, in addition to the plumed busby and frogged hussar tunic, a collar of solid silver several inches deep, presented by George II and considered a regimental treasure of great value. The Regiment was granted the right to keep two drum horses on the strength, but since mechanisation only one remains. For many years the drum horse was a bay, but during the 1960s Princess Margaret presented the Regiment with a magnificent grey, known as 'Crusader', which soon became a universal favourite and set a precedent for grey horses. When the drummer is mounted he wears leather pads on both knees to preserve his uniform from chaffing against the beautiful silver kettle drums. The saddle is covered by a near-perfect leopard skin, while the saddle cloth or shabrack is literally encrusted with battle honours won in three continents. The Regimental badge is a galloping horse, which also features in the Royal Arms of Hanover.

A regular military ceremony in which the horse still plays an outstanding part, is the passing-out parade at the Royal Military Academy, Sandhurst. At one period there were two academies where candidates for the Queen's Commission were trained and educated. One for the cavalry and infantry was at Sandhurst while the artillery and engineers were trained at Woolwich — known as 'The Shop'. The standard of horsemanship was very high at both places, although perhaps higher at Woolwich where gentleman-cadets competed for a saddle of honour.

Woolwich has now closed its doors as a cadet training centre and only Sandhurst remains in this role, although perpetuating the traditions of both academies. The so-called Sovereign's Parade takes place at the end of July before breaking-up, when every cadet and member of staff is expected to be present. It is the last parade before the successful graduates receive their first pip as Subalterns. This follows a strenuous two-year course, which is both academic and practical. The salute is usually taken by the Queen or, if she cannot attend, some other member of the Royal Family.

Drum horse of the Royal Scots Greys c1938.

Drum Sergeant of the 3rd Hussars.

The Sovereign's Parade at Sandhurst.

At first the Colours are trooped between the ranks and a careful inspection is made. Following the march past there is an address of congratulation by the Queen or her representative. Awards are then made to outstanding cadets, including the prized sword of honour and the Monarch's Medal. During the wartime period a belt of honour was substituted for the sword. As a climax the senior cadets march up the broad steps and through the main entrance, followed by the Adjutant on horseback. His charger is usully a magnificent grey with proudly arched neck and flowing mane. Without hesitation he feels his way up the smooth, shallow steps, the light striking on shining spurs, sword and gold braid, before disappearaing into the cool shadows of the great hall. This is a sight to remember and has continued without a break since the founding of the Academy. Even during the wartime period, when cadets were in battledress, the Adjutant still rode his grey, to bring-up the rear, workmanlike and unromantic, in drab khaki.

The Royal Army Veterinary Corps

All animals used by the army, including mascots of all species and large numbers of guard or sniffer dogs, are cared for at some time or other by the Royal Army Veterinary Corps. This unit began as the Army Veterinary Service in 1796, raised to the status of a Royal Corps in 1918, at the close of the Great War. It has served in all parts of the world and taken part in numerous campaigns from the Napoleonic Wars to supporting mounted guerrilla units in the Balkans during the Second World War.

One of its present duties is to purchase and train horses used in the remaining mounted units previously mentioned. Sick and injured horses are tended by skilled veterinary officers attached to separate units, but those seriously hurt or needing special treatment are sent to a centre at Melton Mowbray in Leicestershire.

Recruits joining the corps, after a period of basic training, are then entered for a course of riding and mounted drill, even if their future is intended to be more concerned with dogs than horses. Clerks, storemen, drivers and those involved in the care of sick animals are all taught to control and look after a horse, while recruits showing sufficient promise may advance to more complex courses. Advanced riding for all military personnel was once the domain of the Royal Army Service Corps and later the Royal Corps of Transport, but when the RCT

Horse ambulance c1940, RAVC.

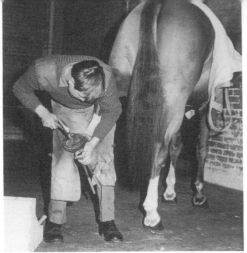

Below left *Rider-grooms with their charges, 1984* (RAVC Depot, Melton Mowbray –
T. Edgson).

Above left *Shoeing a charger in the RAVC School of Farriery* (RAVC Depot, Melton Mowbray
– T. Edgson).

Above right *Army farriers under training* (RAVC Depot, Melton Mowbray – T. Edgson).

was forced to abandon its remaining Animal Transport Companies, this branch
of training was passed to Melton Mowbray. Another interesting feature of the
Melton Mowbray Depot is a school of farriery where soldiers from the RAVC and
other horse-holding units are initiated into the joint arts of blacksmith and
shoeing smith or farrier.

Horses newly arrived as remounts, also those awaiting an intake of recuits or
commencement of an equitation course, need to be fed, groomed and exercised.
This is often the concern of so-called rider-grooms, many of whom are now
members of the Women's Royal Army Corps. These young women are posted to
Melton Mowbray after six weeks at the Guildford Depot of their Corps and taken
on for a probationary period of up to three months. On passing out and electing to
stay with the RAVC, they are usually given the care of one or two horses over a
given period. Others may choose to work in the sick bay and veterinary hospital.
It was here that the equine casualties of the Hyde Park bomb outrage of July 20
1982 were cared for, including the gallant Sefton. Several soldiers and troop
horses suffered death or injury as a result of a terrorist car bomb exploding in the
path of a unit engaged in ceremonial duties.

During the spring of 1984 the author was allowed to visit the Melton Mowbray
Depot and taken on an extensive tour of the lines and quarters. The grouping of
the main buildings, about a mile from the town centre, was in some ways
reminiscent of a farm rather than a military installation. Although some of the
stables dated back to the middle of the last century large numbers were wooden
structures of a prefabricated appearance. There were boxes for about 140 horses,
with extensive grazing on all sides.

We were first conducted through a series of tack and store rooms on the first
floor above some of the older stabling, and shown various types of harness and
equipment, kept for both active service and training purposes. There were

examples not only of saddlery, but of breast harness as used by gun teams and the type of pack gear still being used in the Falkland Islands. Everything was kept in a high state of polish and repair.

The school of farriery, where a charger was being shod and instruction being given, was a long barnlike structure, large enough not to become unbearable in warm weather. There were rows of anvils and glowing forges down one side of the building, echoing to the the welcome clink of metal on metal, while horses awaited attention tethered to the opposite wall — divided from the forge side by a broad gutter. In a room of the adjacent office block was a large showcase containing examples of many different types of shoes used in both military and civil life, especially to correct injuries and imperfections. To the rear of the school was a further low structure, surmounted by a weather vane, showing a model, in profile, of a horse being shod, made by one of the staff as a demonstration piece.

Returning to the stables it was nearing the time for an afternoon feed and many eager heads were craned over half doors, while rider-grooms were busy with their preparations. The horses were all in loose boxes with an automatic water supply for each box. All boxes opened directly into the yard.

In a different part of the stables, behind the covered riding school, an impressive drum horse was being trained for the Life Guards. It is important that such

Below left *Display of horseshoes at the RAVC School of Farriery* (RAVC Depot, Melton Mowbray – T. Edgson).

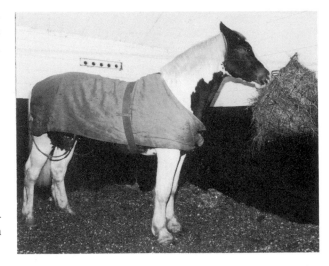

Right *Equine recruit under training* (RAVC Depot, Melton Mowbray – T. Edgson).

animals should learn not only how to move but the correct stance to cope with the unfamiliar weight of elaborate kettle drums. The animal in question was a typical skewbald — brown and white in patches — bred from stock owned by HM The Queen. Yet despite his proud origins he was evidently the paid-up member of a trade union, as he knew his hours of work and was inclined to be less co-operative after a certain time of day.

The stables and horse lines were surrounded by 250 acres of prime grazing shared between horses and cattle. Fields vary from paddocks of four or five acres to meadows of twenty acres and upwards, some with show jumps and jumping lanes, while others have the natural obstacles for a cross country course. It may be noted that while there are upwards of eighty horses at any given time, there are also fifty bullocks kept as store cattle. These latter are sold in the autumn at a reasonable profit to the Corps, having grazed off rank grass left by the more particular horses. A small flock of sheep also appears to have the run of the establishment, increasing its farmlike atmosphere. A few years ago when boilers and heating systems at the depot, now converted to electricity, were fired on solid fuel this was brought from the railhead and factor's yard in wagons drawn by Suffolk Punches, although the last of these have now gone into retirement.

Army horses passing through Melton Mowbray are now mainly bought in Southern Ireland, where remount officers visit a number of farmers and dealers in the breeding areas, especially Waterford. Several months notice may be given to a specific dealer, the purchasing officer arriving at a pre-arranged date and time. A number of horses are brought forward and duly examined in great detail. It may be noted that some of the regular contractors have been connected with this type of work for several generations, running a business that supplies remounts to the British, Irish, Italian and Swiss Armies, among others, and also to leading show jumpers. About forty horses are bought each year by the RAVC, usually in two batches — either three or four years olds, unbroken. Although formerly taken to the docks by road or rail and transferred to the holds of cross-channel steamers, this was far from satisfactory as a few nearly always broke away, especially in rough weather, injuring themselves by slipping down and bumping into solid fittings. They are now boxed in special motor trucks which are driven straight on and off the ships, where they remain until reaching Leicestershire. A few horses are still purchased in England, even sold or donated by private owners, but the majority come from Ireland.

Artillery horses needed by the King's Troop are 15.2 hands high, at least two hands shorter than the minimum for other troop horses. Drum horses needed by the mounted bands of the Household Cavalry have to be skewbalds with their markings following a certain pattern. They are much heavier than ordinary band horses, often with a great deal of feather or fetlock on their heels and lower limbs; this is even more of a tradition in the Life Guards than in the Blues and Royals. A typical drum horse of the Life Guards would not seem out of place in a brewer's dray or coal trolley.

The Army Saddle Club

Although the number of horses in the Army has been greatly reduced there are now better chances for the ordinary soldier to learn riding and stable management than at any time since the First World War. Parachutists, tank drivers, cooks and clerks all have the opportunity to 'feel firm leather under them', through the medium of the Army Saddle Club which is an organisation with branches at most important barracks and camps, teaching men and women to ride on a part-time or hobby basis. This scheme is not so much run by the Army but for the Army, sometimes with civilian instructors and grooms. Serving soldiers are given every encouragement to take part in these activities as riding is an ideal physical exercise, while developing quickness of thought, observation and self-control. Personal tests of activity and endurance on these lines may well be of greater all-round benefit to members of the forces than more conventional team games played in off-duty hours.

During the Great War candidates in the Royal Flying Corps (later the Royal Air Force) for a pilot's course, were often preferred from men with experience of riding and hunting. Riding developed good hands for the control of delicate instruments and a sense of timing. It was also encouraged as an ideal form of relaxation so that a few horses were usually kept on the strength at the larger air bases and flying fields. These facts were gleaned from a combat pilot, serving for nearly three years on the Western Front.

It may be further noted that members of the Household Cavalry stationed in Western Germany have the use of at least twenty horses, frequently transferred from Knightsbridge or Windsor, if only to give them a change from the ardours of ceremonial in a big city. Most of the horses are kept in stables and paddocks at Detmond, hired from civilians, rents paid through the sale of manure to market gardeners. Twelve horses are kept apart from those needed for general purposes, including the odd ceremonial parade, and reserved for special riding courses, which soldiers from any units or of any rank may apply to join. The courses are normally held between September and March. Drag hunting is a popular equestrian sport in this sector.

Cavalry of the Republican Guard of Paris

There are still numerous military units concerned with state ceremonial ranging from the saluting battery of the American Army, based on Fort Meyer, Arlington, in the United States, to the mounted bodyguards of crowned heads and state dignitaries. Some of these may be organised on a volunteer or territorial basis, as in the case of the Saudi-Arabian Cavalry Escort, while most are part of the regular armed forces. Perhaps one of the most outstanding foreign units and certainly one of the most professional, is the Republican Guard of Paris, which may be compared in certain respects to our own Household Cavalry. In other ways it is a unique

Drummer and Trumpeter of the Republican Guard of Paris.

military body, now part of the National Gendarmerie, although in France the police or gendarmerie are an armed corps, quite unlike the civilian forces of the United Kingdom.

The special duties of the Republican Guard relate to the security, defence and internal order of the capital. It escorts the President on ceremonial occasions, while taking a leading part in all important military and state functions. It also acts as a mounted police force in the parks and racecourses of Paris, keeping surveillance over broad tracts of forest-land surrounding the city. In time of war it had contributed a levy of men for campaigns in almost every quarter of the globe, amongst its latest battle honours being Algeria and Indo-China. Those serving in its ranks are all hand-picked men from the French regular army, drawn from career soldiers of non-commissioned status, signing-on for maximum periods of service.

The present guard has a mounted or cavalry regiment, a dismounted or infantry regiment and a squadron of motor cyclists. There is also a mounted band of forty men, taking pride of place on Bastille Day to head a grand parade of the armed forces of the Republic. The cavalry have both duty squadrons and separate training and display units, the latter prominent at public entertainments, shows and galas, also well represented in equestrian sports at international level. They are based on a depot in the Celestine Quarter of the city, where over four hundred horses are stabled, representing four sabre squadrons. This was formerly the site of a mediaeval convent, surrounded by beautiful gardens and extensive grounds.

The mounted regiment is commanded by a Lieutentant Colonel chosen from a serving officer with a distinguished military career and proven skill as an equestrian, having graduated from the Cavalry School of Saumur. On parade the standard or regimental colours is carried by a subaltern, guarded by two adjutants or senior NCOs. These duties are taken turn-and-turn-about so that each man involved has his 'day of honour'. Horses ridden by Standard bearers are usually grey or brown but less frequently chestnut. The Standard of the mounted guard is a square tricolour on a spiked staff, deeply fringed at the borders.

One of the most attractive features of the unit is its distinctive style of uniform, which has changed very little since the reign of Napoleon III. This is roughly the same period from which the present full dress uniform of the British Household Cavalry dates, both appearing as modifications of dragoon or dragoon guard uniforms of the mid-19th century. The French dragoon helmet, very similar to that worn by heavy cavalry of the First Empire (1803–15), is literally its crowing glory and may have been designed by Napoleon I. It is the so-called 'Minerva-type' with an upright crest, based on the helmet worn by the goddess of wisdom, classical allusions having greatly dominated all aspects of art and practical design during the first quarter of the 19th century. The rounded skull-piece is of chromium-plated steel, formerly plain steel with peak, crest and chinscales lined in burnished copper. The plume holder is of solid silver. There is a tuft or streamer of black horsehair while an upright plume is of red cock feathers — the cock being a French national emblem. The helmet of the Commanding Officer has a white aigrette of heron feathers in place of the ordinary plume.

Mounted Honour Guard of the Republican Guard of Paris (ECP Armées).

Band of the Republican Guard of Paris (ECP Armées).

The tunic is black with copper buttons, faced in red with red piping. Skirt flaps are united together in an attractive style, first introduded during the late 17th century, and known as 'a la Soubise'. White riding breeches are worn on full-state occasions, but for less formal duties blue breeches with black stripes at the seams are worn. Boots were traditionally high at the front and cut low at the back but are now replaced by a shorter and more comforable style, originating at the French Cavalry School and known as 'a la Saumur'.

While horses ridden by both officers and men vary in colour, they are matched together in half squadrons, each half squadron known as a peloton. The saddle is of brown leather with a black, red trimmed saddle cloth and holster covers.

As previously mentioned, the pride of the Regiment is the mounted band. Apart from official ceremonial this travels widely and independently in all parts of the country and abroad, visiting horse-shows, public exhibitions and major sporting events, frequently as part of a good-will mission. The first band was raised in 1848 from twelve trumpeters riding chestnut horses, their copper trumpets decorated with fringed banners displaying the arms of Paris and its ancient mural crown. The Republican Guard is perhaps the only military unit in the world to have a full-scale symphony orchestra, frequently augmented by their duty trumpeters when playing classical music that requires extra backing, especially the symphonic poems and Berlioz. The Kettle Drummers do not wear gloves but have gauntlet like cuffs of white, starched material. As with the drum horses of the Household Cavalry there are leather straps or guides leading from bridle to stirrups for leg control at the walk. When playing at the trot, the drummer uses a snaffle bridle with reins in the left hand only, striking the drums alternately with the right hand.

Originally all band horses were chestnuts but since 1955 the colour of drum horses has changed to grey or dappled grey. The present drum banners, known as aprons, show the arms of both Paris and the Republic, and were designed by Lucien Rousselot, official painter to the French Army, a title surviving from the early Napoleonic period. At full-dress parades the trumpet major is flanked by two near-identical drummers, one drum of each set tuned to the trumpets C and G respectively, executing synchronised movements.

Chapter 3

Mounted Police

Introduction
Perhaps some of the least praised and most over-worked public servants in Britain
are the mounted police, yet this fine body has done more to defuse tension and
violence in public places than might be thought possible. Their discrete manner
and impressive bearing adds a touch of dignity to almost any outdoor rally,
demonstration or public festival, often preventing what might deteriorate from
the odd scuffle into mob violence. Crowds of people who are often well-meaning as
individuals are easily swayed in the mass, chanting and gesticulating on the
pavements in ways they would scarcely tolerate either amongst themselves or
their neighbours in a home environment. Ugly scenes may develop from a simple
misunderstanding but, once the mistake occurs its meaning may be exaggerated
out of all proportion, sometimes ending in needless mayhem. Pin-pointing small
incidents and sorting-out genuine trouble-makers from innocent bystanders is

Northumbrian Mounted Police at Roker Park Football Ground, Sunderland (Robert A. Smith).

only a part of mounted police work. In this case the horse provides its rider with a point of vantage and enviable mobility denied the foot police or mechanised constables on motorbikes or in cars.

While crowd control may be achieved with tear-gas, tanks, water cannon and a dozen other modern devices, many of which have been rejected after experiment and discussion, the authorities in most western democracies have no wish to govern by brute force. The intervention of human beings, with spontaneous wit and wisdom, aided by the superior speed and strength of the horse, makes an impact with which voices over loud-speakers or faces behind barriers are unable to compete. The mounted policeman is the human touch with a plus factor. Yet while the man in the saddle is in control, credit is also due to the horses themselves and not least to those who bred and trained them.

A large number of countries have mounted police units and it would seem that the need for them, with the present trends towards over-crowding and mass unemployment, is likely to increase rather than decline, at least during the next half century. Some of the police forces in Continental Europe and North America amount to a branch of the armed services. They are armed and trained like soldiers while their officers have military titles; power often lies in a bulging pistol holster. Such men are obviously capable of using their discretion but the potential of meeting violence with greater violence has no equivalent in the British civilian controlled force, although sometimes to their disadvantage.

London

Perhaps it is in the capital that one is most frequently aware of mounted police. This is partly on account of the numerous demonstrations, ceremonial and sporting events that draw the crowds. It is the home of the Royal Family and centre of Government, all of which requires extra vigilance on the part of the mounted branch. Few people realise that there are two separate police forces in London, both with mounted officers. The larger of the two is the Metropolitan Police with about 200 horses, either mares or geldings, chosen from five basic colours. The City of London Force have a much smaller establishment of seven all-grey geldings, all in a height range between 16.1 and 16.3 hands high. Horses for both units are usually bought in batches, like army remounts, in spring and autumn. Price range is within a fair average but suitable greys, as used in the City, are more expensive on account of their scarcity value. The Metropolitan Police buy roughly 20 horses per year, all of which are trained and schooled at Imber Court in Surrey. This is now one of the most important mounted police training centres in the world, with courses open not only to London officers (both City and Metropolitan) but to those from the provinces and a few from Commonwealth countries and places abroad.

The first London mounted branch dates back to 1758 when, following a period of riot and civil unrest, two mounted officers were attached to the Bow Street Runners, riding what were known as 'swift pursuit horses'. By 1805 there was a regular horse patrol, the terror of highwaymen and footpads, especially at the approaches to the City, where such characters tended to lurk. A so-called flying squad could be sent at short notice to the furthermost ends of the kingdom. By 1836 the mounted patrol was incorporated in the newly formed Metropolitan Police Force. The training centre at Imber Court was opened in 1920, forming part of a programme of intensive reorganisation in all branches and departments. In addition to London, other British centres using horses include Birmingham and the West Midlands, Bristol, Edinburgh, Manchester, Glasgow, Lancashire, Newcastle, Staffordshire, Yorkshire and Liverpool.

Good police horses are of the middle or medium-weight hunter type, now frequently bought in Ireland or Yorkshire. They are noted for good presence and appearance but are also expected to have enough bone for weight-carrying and strenuous work. When purchased they are, for preference, unbroken and unbacked. While chosen as calm and well-balanced they need to be quick in their responses, at home in both a football crowd or at a state function. To become traffic proof is essential, which is partly due to training and partly to character. Riders have to be matched to their horses in outlook and temperament, as a highly strung animal may gain confidence from a placid human, while even a stolid creature may be un-nerved by an edgy, over-sensitive rider. Yet however well-trained, horses, like humans, are unpredictable — at least beyond a certain point. Some develop a fear of a particular vehicle or even the shape of a man's hat, all of which may be traced back to sensible enough explanations and cured. One City of London police horse seemed to dislike open-backed vans, the cause of this relating to a sudden attack from an alsatian dog, guarding parcels in one of them, which horse and rider had unwittingly disturbed.

According to one police officer 'it is harder to retrain than to train', which accounts for a preference for unbroken equine recruits. Both men and horses are expected to go through the mill at Imber Court, many returning for refresher courses at regular intervals.

Most recruits for the mounted police originally came from the cavalry of the line, but since mechanisation they are usually from the suburbs and provincial towns, without much knowledge of horses. The majority learn to ride from scratch although women applicants, now representing ten per cent of the total, are frequently expert riders, perhaps reared in the Pony Club traditions of girlhood. Neither men nor women are considered as direct entries and must have served in other branches of the force before transferring to horses. Because the mounted units are fairly small and self-contained chances for promotion are limited so that applicants must be thoroughly dedicated and sure of themselves. The number of applicants, however, nearly always exceeds the number of vacancies, in every part of the country, which also applies to other jobs with horses.

The first training stint for the London mounted police, at Imber Court, lasts for six months, but only commences after rigorous personal tests, examinations and questioning. Suitability is very much a matter of character and the ability to fit round pegs into round holes. Average height and build are essential and one seldom sees an under-weight, under-height, over-tall or over-weight mounted officer with any force. It is not unusual, however, for applicants to lose at least a stone before the end of training. From the viewpoint of horsemanship the course is even more rigorous than the Household Cavalry, cadets spending at least one and a half hours in the saddle each day from the time of joining. There is troop drill, the basics of dressage (certain movements of which are useful in crowd control) and numerous lectures on stable management, equine anatomy and first aid for both horse and rider. New horses are also trained as part of a six month course, during which they learn how to respond to the aids, jumping in lanes and coping with noises of crowd dispersal or traffic control. As in the Royal Mews and at Knightsbridge Barracks, there are always plenty of rowdies in assorted costumes, banging drums, waving rattles or just yelling their heads off when least expected. Men who never previously rode a donkey on the sands soon find themselves leaping through hoops or negotiating long flights of slippery steps, made from old railway sleepers, on horseback. A great deal of field training involves work with life-sized human dummies, stepping over prone figures or shouldering them out of gateways and under arches without causing serious damage.

After passing out the recruits enter a probationary period, which may last anything from three to twelve months, depending on individual progress. There are nineteen regular stables in the Metropolitan area ranging from Bow to Hampstead. The graduate from Imber is attached to one of these before a permanent posting, exercising the horses of men on leave, filling-in for the sick and injured or just helping with odd jobs around the station.

Police horses are rarely pushed beyond their limits and are always well looked after. With plenty of the right food, care and exercise they lead active lives to a ripe old age, after which they are humanely destroyed. Fourteen to sixteen years in the force is by no means unusual and several horses have been in daily service until they are rising twenty-six. Each year dozens of well-meaning people offer to give a last home or quiet paddock to an ex-police horse, but this is refused as tactfully as possible. Horses living most of their lives in stables, surrounded by noise and activity, only pine away when exiled to half an acre of land and a garden shed.

Horses of the City Force are named after districts of inner London such as Walbrook and Barbican. Metropolitan horses are named according to the year, in alphabetical order, all horses acquired in the same batch having a name beginning with the same letter such as 'Trial', 'Trident', 'Trout', etc.

Birmingham and West Midlands Mounted Police

During March 1984 the author was privileged to visit new stables of the Birmingham and West Midlands Mounted Police in the suburb of Aston. The Commanding Officer responsible for this hospitality was Chief Inspector Duncan Hanna, formerly of the King's Troop, RHA, with whom a personal interview was also granted. A tour of inspection was made, under the guidance of Sergeant Turner, whom it later emerged had been a winner of the annual skill-at-arms trophy, using sword, lance and revolver, in competitions open to all serving members of the armed forces and the police.

Aston Stables were opened at the beginning of 1984 and form part of a £3.5 million complex for the Transportation Department of the West Midland Police

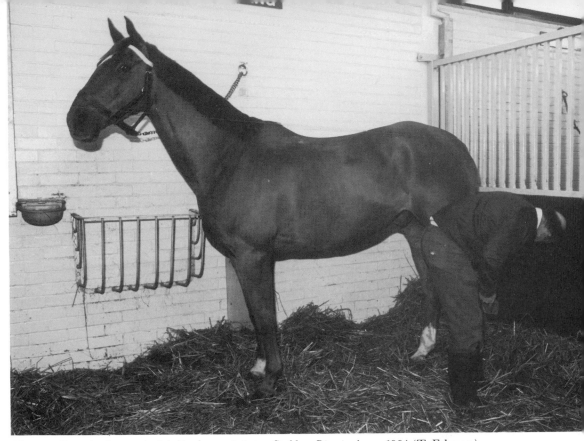

Above *'Lapwing', a typical police horse at Aston Stables, Birmingham, 1984* (T. Edgson).

Below *Aston Police Stables, 1984* (T. Edgson).

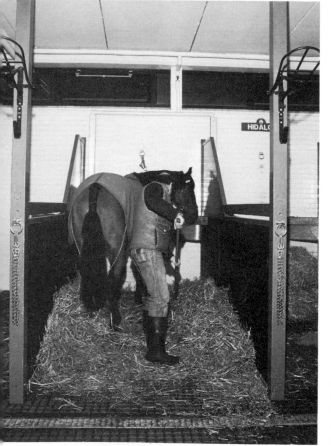

Above left *The Trophy Room, Aston Police Stables. Note the sabres and lances used in ceremonial and the kettle drums in the foreground* (T. Edgson). **Above** *Spare sets of saddlery hanging in the saddle room* (T. Edgson). **Left** *Stable duties — clearing the old bedding out of a stall* (T. Edgson).

Above right *Police Officer grooming his mount using a dandy brush* (T. Edgson). **Above far right** *A farrier shaping an iron fore-shoe with a catshead hammer in the forge of Aston Police Stables* (T. Edgson).

Force. This replaced antiquated buildings in Duke Street, about a mile distant. Compared with life in their former quarters horses were described as now 'living in the lap of equine luxury'. The modern structure is grouped on three sides of an inner reservation, surrounded by a continuous exercise track. At the northern end were offices while on the right were tack or harness rooms, a trophy room and further administrative quarters. The southern end of the building was occupied by the stable block proper, with spacious stalls and a few loose boxes on either side of a central gangway. Smaller horses were kept in stalls and larger horses in boxes, each stall and box fitted with an automatic watering system. At the far end of the stalls was a shoeing forge in which two men were hard at work, one of them — a cheerful Scot predictably named Jock — was pushing seventy-seven and shrugged-off any suggestions that he might retire and take things easy. Joe Larkin, an ex-champion jockey who rode a hundred and twenty winners and is now attached to the stables, claimed the place was a real show piece. . . . 'definitely one of the finest stables I have ever seen.'

Arriving shortly after 9 am we were in time to see a mounted patrol parade for briefing just as they were about to set out, leaving stables in single file to find their individual beats in busy streets or quiet parks and suburbs. Ordinary patrols are about 15–16 miles. In addition to run-of-the-mill or public order jobs Saturdays are noted for their involvement in sporting activities, especially during the football season, at both St Andrew's Ground and Villa Park. At one time there were hectic scenes and traffic jams to control at Birmingham Racecourse, but this has now closed to make way for housing development. Sunday is normally a day of rest.

Horses for the Birmingham and West Midlands Force have to be purchased within a competitive price range, acquired from reputable dealers. They are normally about 16 hands high, although some younger animals may be slightly smaller but expected to gain height in service. Most are bought between the ages of four and six, seldom much older, and serve for an average of 15 years. In 1923 the Birmingham City Police Force had 23 horses. The force was amalgamated with the West Midlands Area Police in 1974, giving the combined force a grand total of 54 horses, including extra horses as remounts. There are 29 at the Aston stables while others are kept at West Bromwich and other centres. Horses detained after dark, on winter duties, wear fluorescent gaiters or leg coverings and stirrup lamps.

Recruits applying to join the West Midlands Mounted Branch must have served in the local force for a minimum of two years. They are expected to be fit, healthy and weigh in the region of 12 stone. Successful applicants are trained at the 'Tally Ho' Police Headquarters, Edgbaston, which is also the remount depot and sick bay. The course lasts nine weeks and ends with both practical and written examinations. There are numerous lectures on veterinary matters, stable management and many other things concerning horses. Not least of the subjects to be covered is the care and cleaning of kit as a smart turnout is essential for self-respect and to earn the respect of the public in general. Before posting to active duties each new constable is given a personal inspection and practical riding test by the Chief Inspector. Early street patrols are made in the company of a Police Sergeant or Senior Constable. Mounted policemen are expected to treat themselves and their horses for minor ailments and injuries, calling in doctor or vet only in extreme circumstances.

The complete set of saddlery is expected to last a great many years (including the sword stick), now costing upwards of £600 per kit. The sword stick is frequently attached to the pommel or front of the saddle, but seldom used. It is basically a metal rod in a wooden case and far less dangerous than the flat of a sabre, widely used by continental police forces. It may be noted that the Liverpool and several other forces use a considerable amount of ex-War Department saddlery, most of this acquired at the time of widespread mechanisation, during the late 1930s. The Birmingham and West Midlands Force retain both sabres and lances for ceremonial purposes and musical rides, also for practise in the skill-at-arms competitions previously mentioned.

The following notes are based on instruction sheets available to all personnel of the mounted branch at Aston Headquarters:

Hints when on Mounted Patrol

a. When anticipating a long tour of duty, dismount and loosen the girth at every opportunity.

b. Do not allow the horse to go long without food, even a handful or two of grass is a great help.

c. Always carry a feed when your hour of return to stables is uncertain.

d. Do not give a horse fast work after a bulky feed.

e. If on a long journey an occasional trot will help ease the horse's back.

f. Reserves in open spaces, such as parks, should be drawn-up in line, if possible away from the general public.

g. Horses should not be tethered in a police station yard and left unattended whilst the officer is handing in a report at the office. Every endeavour should be made to obtain another officer to hold the mount.

h. Travel single file in narrow lanes and narrow or congested streets.

i. Avoid, if possible, using horses in crowds or at functions where children predominate.

j. If a horse that is usually placid suddenly becomes fretful, examine saddlery and search the mouth for bit injuries.

k. Excessive sluggishness on patrol is often a symptom of disease and the fact should be reported as soon as possible.

The Royal Canadian Mounted Police

This is one of the most spectacular mounted police units in the world, symbolising all that is most attractive in the extreme northern part of the American Continent. Countless travel posters showing a mounted officer scanning vast horizons, have drawn both tourists and settlers to sample the possibilities of a new world through this medium.

Slightly more than a century ago the RCMP was formed to guard and patrol vast territories in Northern Canada ceded to the Government by the Hudson Bay Company. Their duties were to keep order, enforce the collection of customs dues and stamp out an illicit traffic in hard liquor, the abuse of which might have led to serious Indian risings. The courage and fortitude of these men, in a frequently hostile environment, became legendary, inspiring songs, verses, novels and even the celebrated operetta 'Rose Marie'.

Royal Canadian Mounted Police at the Coronation of Elizabeth II (The Field).

Originally known as the Canadian North West Mounted they changed their title to the Royal Canadian Mounted Police in 1920, perhaps leading to some confusion as there are separate and still flourishing units of mounted police under local administration in several parts of the country. The duties and jurisdiction of the present RCMP, however, are nationwide, spanning provincial boundaries from maritime settlements and islands to the Pacific coast and sparsely settled lands within the Arctic Circle.

While modern RCMP make use of motor cycles, speed boats, motorised sledges and even light aircraft, there is still a mounted branch in the conventional sense of the word, based in the Canadian capital. This appears on most state occasions and provides horses and men for the celebrated musical ride, performed in a number of countries, especially Canada, Great Britain and the United States. The RCMP and their predecessors have sent mounted contingents to coronations and jubilees in London since the Victorian era. In 1973, during a royal tour of Canada, the Queen made a special visit of inspection to the mounted police headquarters in Ottawa, which coincided with the year of their centenary. At the end of the ceremonial and traditional march past Her Majesty was presented with a magnificent black thoroughbred named 'Centennial', for her personal use. The Queen has also received the thoroughbred mare 'Burmese', as a further gift from the 'mounties', which she frequently rides side saddle, at the Trooping of the Colour ceremony, to mark her official birthday. All horses used by the RCMP are black in colour, tending to darken with age. They are now mostly bred on their official stud farm at Pakenham, Ontario.

The musical ride, based on elements of the cavalry drill book set to music, is performed by a troop of 32 men, all volunteers and enthusiasts. Learning the complicated figures takes each man and horse a period of over three months' hard work. The mounties enter the arena or parade ground in review uniforms with scarlet tunics, blue breeches, brown riding boots and broad-brimmed felt hats, the latter designed by a member of the force in 1905 to replace a less practical pillbox cap. Saddles are of the 'colonial' type, intended for Empire service, with a saddle cloth of dark blue, having yellow borders and the letters 'CMP' in each of the corresponding corners. For the ride bamboo lances with steel tips are carried, which, like the red tunics, are said to have made a great impression on the native Indians. To the Indian tribes red was the colour of bravery while the lance was a token of honour and leadership. Each lance has a red and white pennon to flutter in the breeze, crimped in a traditional style to commemorate acts of courage in which similar pennons were dipped and stiffened in the blood of the enemy. The lance is now a ceremonial weapon but plays an essential part in the musical ride, especially in forming what is known as 'The Wedding Arch'. Other movements are known as 'The Star', 'The Maze' and 'The Dome', but none are more spectacular than 'The Shanghi Cross', with four sets of eight men cantering towards each other from opposite corners of the arena. At the end of each ride there is a simulated charge at full gallop, the front rank riding with lowered lances. Other movements of the ride are enacted with raised lances at the trot or canter.

One of the official duties of the RCMP is to drive and care for the National State

Carriage, which is used on many ceremonial occasions. This is now minus the box seat, like the Gold State Coach of England, and controlled by two mounted drivers wearing full review uniforms and escorted by lancers. The hood is usually kept open when the Queen or Governor-General are driving in Ottawa, but raised when foreign ambassadors or other dignitaries are passengers.

The carriage has a long and varied history. It was assembled during the Victorian era, at the coach and carriage works of Ewing Brothers in Melbourne, Australia, although most of the iron-work was shipped out by a Birmingham firm. It is a canoe landau with curved rather than square sides, originally driven from a high box seat. It was first used by Lord Hopetoun, a former Governor-General of Australia. At the end of his period of office his lordship returned to England, taking the carriage with him. It was eventually sold to Earl Grey, the newly appointed Governor-General of Canada. On his retirement in 1911, Earl Grey presented it to the Canadian Government. This, however, was approaching the age of the motor car and in 1926 the State Carriage was retired as a museum-piece. It was returned to service at the behest of Governor-General Ian Massey, renowned for his love of ceremonial, and fully restored in 1970–71. When not in use the vehicle is on public display at Divisional Headquarters ('N' Division) in Ottawa.

Horses used in ceremonial drives are at least 16 hands high and move at a rapid trot. Their timing, like the old mail coaches, is almost to a split second. They are matched for gait, height, colour and general appearance, trained in both ridden and driven duties. Preparing the carriage and harness, and the equipment of the postilions and escort, takes at least two full days.

The New York City Police

There are mounted police units and rangers in many parts of the United States, the largest and most efficient being in New York City. This has at least a third more horses than the London police with 150 stabled in the 22nd Precinct alone, which includes Manhattan's Central Park. Yet in addition to park patrols, New York City Police are widely involved in traffic problems, a serious headache for the community over half a century. In addition to more than its share of both vehicles and pedestrians, traffic flow in the central areas has long been hampered by moving bridges, street railways and unguarded level-crossings, all of which need special surveillance by mounted men. The mounted policeman also serves as a species of traffic warden, handing out tickets for parking offences and checking other misdemeanours.

Central Park was designed as early as 1857 by the architects Olmsted and Vaux. An area of preserved and manicured rather than natural beauty, it contains a riding school, boating lakes, children's play areas and its own zoo. Hackney carriages ply for hire, each with a single horse between shafts, while there is also a certain amount of pleasure riding, as in London's Hyde Park. Although an important centre for tourists and leisure seekers it has acquired, in recent years, an unsavoury reputation as an under-cover meeting place for drug addicts and petty criminals of all types. This means constant awareness and tactful supervision on the part of mounted officers.

When new police stables were needed it was decided to build them in the park and, to avoid spoiling local amenities, they were constructed underground. The same scheme now includes a blacksmith's shop, forage stores, garages and a public stable, in addition to police quarters, only a small part of which is showing above ground level. The contract was handled by the firm of Gruzen and Partners, leading to considerable redesigning and replanting at one end of the park, but at least preserving open spaces and living greenery in the heart of one of the most densely populated urban areas in the world.

Looking to the future

Whatever the fate of other horses in national and commercial usage the police horse is likely to remain an important animal for many years to come. The motor vehicle is now not so much a rival but a worthy ally and where there is serious local unrest squads of mounted police may be boxed-up and rushed to the spot, sometimes well outside the area, in record time. It is said that many town dwellers, especially younger people, are sometimes overawed by the presence of horses — no longer familiar in every-day life. This uncertainty and the chance for an odd gleam of humour (such as 'move back if you please ... he won't tread on your toes if you don't step on his') may even prove a useful asset in breaking tension and dispersing a crowd. Many policemen now wear helmets for crowd control, especially useful when stones and other missiles are thrown at random. Horses may be issued with protective blinkers in the form of plastic eye-shields.

Chapter 4

Entertainment and promotions

Horses have appeared in public entertainment for thousands of years, perhaps as long as they have been domesticated. Chariot racing in hippodromes was one of the great spectacles of Ancient Rome, although previously practised by the Greeks and Etruscans as a form of military training. Throughout the Middle Ages and later periods performing horses and those trained in the rigours of classical horsemanship were always popular with discerning audiences. At fairs, and later with small travelling shows, the educated horse, able to spell its name in bricks or cards, a task often beyond the skill of many people in the audience, was a star performer. Responding to pre-arranged signals it could answer highly amusing questions concerning public figures, merely by nodding its head or stamping a fore-hoof.

The sawdust ring

It was in the circus that horses first achieved higher levels of recognition as entertainers, although human riders and presenters frequently claimed most of the credit. Even today the circus is unthinkable without horses and attempts at staging shows with only human performers, is like *Hamlet* without the Prince of Denmark.

Although modern circus depends on international performers from both sides of the Atlantic, it is firmly based on English traditions and was introduced by a former riding instructor in a British cavalry regiment, known as Philip Astley. His first circus, however, was a permanent show on the banks of the Thames in Lambeth, dating from the second half of the 18th century, being a sawdust ring surrounded by tiers of fixed seating. The first tenting or touring circus was the idea of a Frenchman known as Franconi, who lived to be nearly a hundred, and is also credited with the invention of the caravan or house-on-wheels, indispensible for modern travelling shows.

Circuses and equestrian displays soon caught the imagination of the upper classes — especially those with hidden talents and unlimited leisure. Men from ancient and highly respected families joined the circus as performers on long or short term engagements, many being former military officers, so that very soon every bare-back rider or animal trainer was a Captain, Major or Colonel — if frequently self-promoted! It is a well-known fact that Queen Victoria staged private circus acts in a courtyard at Windsor Castle, presented by the Sangers and other leading showmen of the day. Some of the most attractive riding displays at the two permanent circuses in Paris were presented by society ladies, while the Empress Elizabeth of Austria trained a pair of spotted horses named 'Flick' and 'Flock', and presented a high school act on her famous thoroughbred 'Avolo'. Amateur shows were frequently held by the Empress in the Imperial Riding School at Gödölö.

Towards the end of the 19th century there were several Wild West Shows, touring in both America and Europe, based on the original show of that name staged by Colonel William Codey or 'Buffalo Bill', formerly Chief Scout of the American Army. This type of entertainment was not perhaps true circus, performed in a rectangular arena rather than a sawdust ring, but had much in common with other tenting shows of its day. It was renowned not only for roping, shooting and bronco-busting by frontiersmen but for an International Congress of Rough Riders, in which skilled horsemen from the deserts of Central Asia to the pampas of South America took part.

The Forty Horse Hitch and the World Circus Museum
A notable feature of all circus and wild west shows was the big parade, held a few hours before the first opening. This would be headed by the band wagon and various tableaux trucks or floats, drawn by large teams of horses, the vehicles richly carved and painted, driven with consummate skill. Perhaps the best known of these wagons and teams was the celebrated 'Forty Horse Hitch', which was re-created for the Circus World Museum, Baraboo, Wisconsin, in 1972.

Horse-drawn band wagon.

The present Circus Museum, where full dress parades, acts in the sawdust ring and informal training sessions are on daily show to the public, also includes a remarkable collection of horse-drawn caravans, steam organs, beast cages and other types of equipment, many over a century old. Baraboo was formerly the winter quarters of the Ringling Brothers, who later amalgamated with the Barnum and Bailey Circus, sharing new quarters with the older show at a site in Connecticut.

The Baraboo centre with its stables, wagon building shops, shoeing forges and whole wardrobes of expensive costumes was restored through the interest of John M. Kelly, a great enthusiast for the tenting circus. He had worked for the Ringling Brothers not, however, as a performer or ring-master but as a legal adviser, settling claims caused by accidents encountered on even the best conducted tours. His particular enthusiasm was the Forty Horse Hitch, formerly the pride of the show.

It may be of interest to record that on the first appearance of the Hitch in England disaster was crowned by unexpected success. While driving through a narrow street in King's Lynn, a slight error in turning caught a projecting window and ripped off the frontage of a local hotel. Fortunately there were no serious injuries and the accident brought much-needed publicity to the house, eventually renamed and flourishing as 'The Forty Horse Inn'. More than 60 years later the Forty Horse Hitch again took the road, mainly due to the efforts and imagination of J. M. Kelly, supported by a director and restoration expert at the museum, known as Charles P. ('Chappie') Fox. They were further assisted, on the financial side, by the International brewing concern of Jos Schlitz and Company, whose President was an enthusiast for all types of harness horses. A revived version of the Circus Parade was held in the main streets of Milwaukee on Independence Day (4th July), which was a public holiday, drawing crowds of 400,000 people. There were clowns, performing animals, acrobats and jugglers but the magnificent teams of Belgian draught horses were the real stars of the show. This was during the 1960s and the parade has been repeated on many other occasions as a summer spectacular.

Apart from performing and ridden horses, every traditional circus needed large teams of 'heavies' both for transport and hauling on pulley-ropes to raise the big top. Even when the show was taken between centres by train, horses were required to assist in off-loading the wagons and taking them to the show ground, perhaps a mile or so from the nearest railhead. Percherons, Belgians and even Clydesdales were used in this work, usually in matching teams. The Milwaukee parades, aided by the Circus Museum and the Schlitz Breweries, have now become something of a national event. In 1972, apart from the Forty Horse Hitch, the gallant Belgians harnessed four abreast, there were about 750 horses, ponies and mules, including 325 teams of matching draught horses hauling 70 parade wagons.

The circus in Europe
The circus is certainly well established in America, also in most parts of

Continental Europe, on both sides of the Iron Curtain. While it is obviously a matter of free enterprise in Western Countries the Eastern bloc have state circuses and national training academies where budding performers are given the chance to study and develop their arts. Fortunately for circus performers, international barriers are low and there is still considerable interchange of acts and ideas between states that are normally divided from each other by rival politics and ideologies.

Some of the finest natural horsemen in Eastern Europe are the Cossacks, descended from a race of semi-nomadic herdsmen, dominated by their elected leaders or hetmen. While fighting mainly for the Russians, especially in Czarist times, large contingents have also served under Polish and Turkish flags. Now mainly settled on Russian territory, where many continue to guard and patrol their herds of wild horses, they frequently entertain their fellow countrymen with thrilling acts of riding, acrobatics and marksmanship. After the period of civil wars following the Revolution of 1917, however, several groups decided to leave Russia and tour Western countries with trick-riding and equestrian displays, some of which could be seen in Britain up to the early 1960s. The author has vivid

Cossack trick rider.

memories of such acts with teams of chanting horsemen riding in living pyramids or clustered, like a star burst, round a symbolic flag.

The main Russian centre for circus riding and training is the Equestrian Academy at Ivanovo, formerly under the direction of the world-renowned horse-man Alexandrov. This has relied to a considerable extent on Cossack riders, especially the Kalganov Troupe of dare-devil horsemen, controlled by a mounted, whip cracking ringmaster, and the Alexandrov Serge bare-back riders who perform continuous backward somersaults on files of cantering horses.

There are about fifteen circuses in Great Britain, a further five in Ireland and also two resident circuses during the summer season at Blackpool Tower and Great Yarmouth Hippodrome, with winter circuses at Glasgow, Manchester and two or three other centres. The annual Christmas Circus at Bingley Hall, Birmingham (the first permanent, purpose-designed exhibition hall in the world, pre-dating the Crystal Palace), may not appear for a further season as its venue was destroyed by fire during the winter of 1984.

Full details of the above shows appear in the Annual Circus Directory of the British Isles published each year as part of the September issue of 'King Pole', the magazine of the flourishing 'Circus Fans Association of Great Britain', obtainable from David Davis, 8 Casslee Road, Catford, London SE6 4XH.

Types of act and their horses

During a visit to the Chipperfield Circus at Bingley Hall, shortly before the end of their last Christmas season, the author was fortunate to have been granted an interview by James Clubb, the husband and chief animal trainer of Sally Chipperfield. Many of the following details relating to horses in the circus are drawn from his remarks and conversation. There are now two separate branches of the world famous Chipperfield Circus, one run by Sally and the other by her sister Mary. It may be noted that the Chipperfields have been in entertainment and showmanship since the reign of Charles II and are perhaps the oldest circus family in Britain.

The two main categories in which horses appear at a modern circus are the ridden acts and the unridden or liberty acts. The most advanced or sophisticated type of work, nearest the standards of classical horsemanship, is high school riding or haute école. Yet despite occasional television programmes covering this art, with visits not only to shows in England but to centres abroad, such as the Spanish Riding School at Vienna, it seems this form of riding is less interesting to the average audience than in former days. It is an act for the connoisseur with an intimate knowledge of horses, while for the layman it must be tricked-out with bright costumes and just the right effects of music and lighting to make it interesting. When presented by a woman this type of act was frequently ridden side saddle. It is still performed with style and elegance by several exponents including Katja Schumann of Denmark, a member of the Schumann family who have been noted for their riding and liberty acts for three or more generations. Other similar acts frequently appear at the Circus Knie in Switzerland, including a family tandem number, in which horses are both ridden and driven. Other

Left *Circus act in training.*

Below *James Clubb of Sally Chipperfield's Circus showing a liberty horse* (David Jamieson).

Below right *Modern circus act using a Russian bred stallion* (David Jamieson).

riding acts, perhaps more exciting but less sophisticated, are considered in a further part of this chapter.

Liberty acts are performed by troupes of horses worked together without riders, ranging from pairs or threes to a dozen. A much larger number would be difficult to control, on a regular basis, in the circus ring, although fine acts have appeared with sixteen horses these were exceptions, depending on smaller horses than average. The horses perform intricate figures within the ring but frequently stand with their fore or hind legs on the walkway at the circumference of the ring, according to training. The presenter of the act usually wears evening dress or a formal type of costume and carries a whip or sometimes two whips, according to tradition. These may be cracked and raised, not to injure or frighten the horses but to use as signals. Only light harness is worn with side or check reins to prevent the horse tossing its head about. These connect the bridle with a back-band and have been criticised as over-strict, but are comfortable enough for short periods and are only worn in the ring. It is essential that a liberty horse should catch the presenter's eye as without restraint it might be inclined to toss its head and lose concentration, not only spoiling the act but leading to dangerous confusion.

While the ridden horse for high school acts may be a stallion or mare, stallions

are definitely preferred for liberty work. The male entire seems to have a better sense of team spirit and concerted action than mares or geldings, without sacrificing individuality. They are not likely to turn sour or cunning, which would be a great bugbear during training sessions. In the ring entires act together with greater harmony than mares or geldings, even if likely to attack each other in stables or paddocks, if not restrained. Although spending a considerable part of their time in close proximity during the touring season and training sessions, it is unwise for more than one stallion to be left in each field or paddock at the winter quarters.

Arabs or Anglo-Arabs (a cross between an Arab and an English Thorough-bred) are preferred for liberty work, although in modern times the spotted Knabstrup and sometimes the slightly heavier Fresian may be used. Horses are considered more difficult to train than other animals because of their individual and sensitive natures, rather than through natural stubbornness or stupidity. It is necessary to establish a good relationship between horse and trainer and to work through patience and kindness. With the right approach the active, healthy horse soon begins to take a pleasure in learning and even shows impatience to begin his work sessions. Praise and rewards are the only mediums through which an act may become successful and visually worthwhile. It might be possible to use fear and pain but the results would seem lifeless and devoid of true meaning or artistry. Employees at the Circus Knie in Switzerland have been sacked on the spot for merely slapping a horse in anger.

Arab horses learn quickly and are more tractable than most breeds. They may be bought at the ages of three or four years old, towards the end of the summer, and are good enough to appear at a major Christmas circus by mid-December. During part of that time they may be with a tenting show, not in permanent stables but spending only a few days in familiar quarters, each town divided from the next by hours of travel and confusion. The Arab also has a good conformation and presence, qualities which are ideal for showmanship. Most are between 14.1 and 15 hands high, a convenient size when several appear together. Larger horses such as Anglo-Arabs and Hanoverians usually appear in smaller numbers than Arabs. English Thoroughbreds are now considered too highly strung and excitable for the sawdust ring, although a few may be trained for high school riding or single acts under the supervision of a single person with individed attention. Several acts, in recent years, have been presented with mixed teams of horses, ponies and even zebras. Such performances however, apart from their novelty value, lack the charm, grace and intricacy displayed by well-bred, matching horses of single breed.

An amusing act sponsored by Mary Chipperfield is known as 'Big and Little' in which a gigantic Shire or Clydesdale appears with a miniature Shetland Pony, the smaller animal running between the legs of its stable mate. 'Big and Little' is reminiscent of an earlier act known as 'Walking the Pony' in which a tiny Shetland lay on the ground while larger horses walked over it in procession. It would then rise to its feet and rush after the other animals only to overtake them and lie down in front of their leader, continuing the routine as long as the act

Above *Walking the pony*.

Below *A 'Big and Little' act, 1984* (David Jamieson).

Left *A bareback riding act*
(David Jamieson).

Below *The Richter Bareback
Riding Family from Hungary*
(David Jamieson).

Right *Natural dignity.*

lasted. A 'Big and Little' act prepared by Carlo MacManus frequently uses a Clydesdale known as Oliver Reed, having been purchased from the private stables of the well-known film actor.

Shetland ponies frequently appear in the circus ring or on the stage with performing dogs. Dogs learn to ride ponies and leap on to their backs either from tubs or ground level, sometimes from high steps. Monkeys have been used in place of dogs but do not prove such rewarding material, partly on account of their physical structure. In some modern shows, especially in North America, individual horses have learned to overcome their natural fear and dislike of the big cats and it is no longer unusual to see a lion or tiger riding not bare-back, but on a specially padded saddle cloth. A similar act was performed in the tenting Circus of Bertram Mills, during the mid 1930s, the rather cross-grained horse being more dangerous and harder to handle than the tiger. Almost anything may be achieved with the right control and temperament, although any suggestion of bullying and excessive noise are the worst enemies of modern showmanship. Whenever possible movements in the ring should be clearly defined, natural and above all dignified. Horses, or any other animals, squatting on their haunches and wearing top hats or cricket caps merely for a cheap laugh are subjects for ridicule rather than admiration and should not be allowed to suffer such indignities.

While Arabs, Anglo-Arabs, Hanoverians and sometimes Lipizzaners are preferred for liberty and more conventional riding acts, there is a further category of performance in which a heavier and perhaps coarser type of animal takes the limelight. This is the stocky, broad-beamed Rosinback, frequently used for bare-back riding, harmless resin or rosin being rubbed on the place where the saddle normally rests, to give its rider a better foothold. These acts are said to be more difficult than so-called Cossack riding as much of the mounted work is performed in a standing position with scarcely anywhere to hold or grip. The Cossack at least has a saddle, although in fairness to Cossacks these riders often discard their saddles at full gallop or ride on uncovered parts of the horse, such as neck or withers, in a reversed position. It is essential, however, that the mounts of most bare-back riders should be steady and docile, with a comfortable rather than a spectacular gait. Such animals may be either mares or geldings and are usually crossbred. A few have even begun their careers on the streets, pulling milk floats or bread vans.

While some Rosinbacks canter round the ring as singles others appear as three and four abreast rotating in a pin-wheel effect, the horse on the inside moving much slower and a shorter distance than those further out. Notable exponents of these acts, among others, are the Enrico Caroli family from Italy and the Zapachay Brothers of the Moscow State Circus, the latter riding on ex-farm horses. These are not so much displays of fine horsemanship but acrobatics on horseback. Martine Gruss of the Cirque Gruss in France has a far more tradi-tional act in which all movements are based on the classical ballet.

During the past few years the larger and more powerful types of draught horses have sometimes appeared in acts normally associated with lighter weight and more elegant breeds. East German trainer Herman Ullmann has experimented with brauereipferde or brewery dray horses in groups of six, many of the movements being on the hind legs, an awesome and impressive but not perhaps a graceful sight. Acts in which heavyweights appear, although revived in popularity since the Second World War, are not always breaking new ground but have a particular appeal for the Americans, Germans and other Northern Europeans. One of the largest horse acts ever staged, in a slightly larger than average ring, was a mixed troupe of Fresians with Arabs, Oldenburghers and Lipizanners up to sixty in number, handled by master-trainer Althoff, much earlier in the century. Mary Chipperfield has also presented mixed troupes of two Clydesdale horses, two ponies and both African and Asian elephants.

Other entertainers

Circuses are not the only forms of modern entertainment in which horses take part. Many appearing at outdoor shows and fetes throughout the country, offer displays of trick riding and driving independent of the Big Top. There are often reconstructions of Wild West Shows, early chariot racing and tournaments or jousting — the latter popular as a royal sport from the Middle Ages to the mid 17th Century.

One of the leading exponents of such activities is the expatriat Frenchman Gerard Naprous, based on a location in rural Shropshire, where he has the lease of

Above *Gerard Naprous driving one of his Roman chariots in rehersal at his home in Shropshire* (Gerard Naprous).

Below *The start of a Roman chariot race at a show in South Wales* (South Wales Evening Post).

a large stable block adjacent to the Manor of Loton Hall, surrounded by several hundred acres of grazing and parkland. Gerard was born in Paris, neither of his parents being involved with horses or even animal lovers. He is said to have greatly shocked them by planning to seek work as a groom, undeterred by the long hours and rigours of mucking out on cold mornings. It was not long before he had risen to become a professional coachman, working for a firm that specialised in filming and promotions. This gave him the opportunity to tour widely and observe many local tricks and methods of training, becoming adept as both a stunt rider and driver. For a time he was with a circus in Spain, appearing in a Wild West Act that served as a pipe-opener to the main show. Returning to Paris he was accepted as a member of an internationally famous stunt team, with engagements at the Paris Lido. A further engagement brought him to Britain and an exhibition of jousting at the Blackpool Opera House, as part of the Ken Dodd Spectacular.

He now runs his own team which specialises in mock-chariot racing, the vehicles being of his own construction and design, often using the discarded artillery wheels of former pack batteries, which have now been replaced, in the British Army, by disc-wheels with pneumatic tyres. Gerard has also personally built a replica of a Concord or Western-type stage coach, used in some of his acts and for training purposes. This is constructed entirely from metal sheeting, rather than wood, leather and iron, and stands-up better to high-speed driving and buffeting of the showground than conventional materials.

Ridden and driven horses of Gerard's troupe are all trained to a high pitch of perfection, climbing stairs, shamming dead and leaping through hoops at a word of command. The highlight of his productions, however, is always the Roman Chariot Race, in which there are feigned accidents and wheels drop off in a most convincing manner. Driving hell-for-leather, far removed from the controlled British methods, there is more dash and daring than sheer elegance, for which he is known as 'The Flying Frenchman' and his troupe as 'les cavaliers du diable' — horsemen of the devil.

Gerard is renowned for his highly successful training methods and the devotion of his horse teams. He praises and rewards their efforts and they work even harder to earn his gratitude. Given the right circumstances he can train an unbroken horse to show standard in a fortnight — but this is far from ideal. Most of the animals he uses are of Arab blood but many are also Welsh Cobs or from Welsh stock, being both willing and intelligent. Most of his horses are bought unbacked and unbroken, either through reputable dealers or at sales. Few of his horses are more than 15 hands high and he claims that, in general terms, smaller animals are not only handier but quicker to learn and less troublesome in training.

Since the Second World War several British troupes or teams have been involved in exhibition jousting and mock tournaments. There has even been the foundation of a British Jousting Society, responsible for displays of mounted skills in the mediaeval tradition at shows, fetes and festivals, also hiring out teams and individuals for television and filming. The men who first inspired these activities were two stunt riders from the film industry known as 'Nosher' Powell and Max Diamond, their organiser and manager was Brigadier Peter Young (known as the

'Knight Marshal'). The team eventually included several other stunt men and trick riders, with ten knights champion and a deputy marshal of the lists — keeping order and helping to run the show with clockwork precision. Other 'back-up' members of the group included grooms, truck drivers, wardrobe staff and a stable manager. Fourteen horses were made available for each show.

Jousting has always been a dangerous sport, especially in its earlier forms, with fractures, heavy bruises and painful lacerations. None of these can be faked, as often happens in the films or on television by trick photography. Yet damage and injury happens to the men who take part and seldom to the horses, both through skilful riding and the nature of the activity.

For public performances in the modern idiom, jousting or tilting is based on 12th century practise, with light chain mail worn under colourful surcoats of heraldic design, the head enclosed by a rounded but flat-topped jousting helm or helmet. During the later Middle Ages plate armour was preferred, much heavier than chain mail but well-padded internally; the horses were also larger, to carry greater weight, and the action was much slower. Horses and riders now charge at each other at full gallop from opposite ends of a barrier or tilt, from which the expression 'going full tilt' must have derived. The aim is to strike the opponent in the middle of his shield, to unhorse or disarm him, at an impact of between fifty and sixty miles per hour. While the lances are always blunt-ended, they are about 12 ft long and are capable of considerable damage. By slipping or missing the target area they may prove lethal.

Horses have to be fairly large for this type of work, with plenty of fire and determination, but also good temperament for working in crowds and noisy surroundings. The right sort is often a cross between a Cleveland Bay and a Thoroughbred.

Filming and the theatre

Not all horses used in filming and television are war horses or military chargers, although this might account for large numbers of them. Many, as might be expected, are the broncos of cowboys, Indians and other western characters, while others pull carts and carriages in the background or pass through the set as if being led to and from stables. In a BBC television production of Jane Austen's *Mansfield Park* the heroine journeyed to Portsmouth in a beautiful travelling chariot with a pair of matching carriage horses. These and other horses and carriages were hired from D. J. Goodey of the Foxhill Stables near Reading, a firm widely involved in film work with historical backgrounds.

There are many firms and individuals throughout Britain, Europe and North America supplying horses for filming, while others also provide trained stunt riders or drivers. One of the largest stables for this type of work in Britain is operated by a Mr Wicks (senior) of Westonbirt, in Wiltshire. He has provided horses for productions as widely different as *The Canterbury Tales* and *The Invisible Man*. Horses and coaches may be taken long distances for location-work, in special horse boxes which may also serve as temporary stabling. Mr Wicks, in addition to his film and television work, runs the Bath Carriage Museum and is

Private cab c1930.

now the last contractor in the country able to provide the right type of horses and mourning carriages for a full-scale horse funeral. The horses are all-black Gelderlanders, imported from Holland. Horse funerals were still popular in Ireland during the 1960s and 70s but have recently been phased out.

All the main Hollywood studios have made numerous westerns and historical romances, some even known as 'horse operas', in which four-legged performers have earned as much applause as the people riding them. Trained animals, like young children, frequently steal the show and horses are nearly always star material, if presented in the right way. Some of the best films of this type, with high box-office potential and suitable as all-round family entertainment, have been produced by the Walt Disney organisation. A large number of these were made by Larry Lansburgh, noted not only as a film-maker but as a highly skilled horseman and a regular judge on the panel of the American Horse Show Association. He frequently films sequences while riding alongside other galloping horses, with a ciné camera strapped to a shoulder rest of his own invention.

Fortunately the days have now passed in which horses were made to drop, in mock battles, by the use of concealed trip wires and pitfalls. Trainers such as Lansburgh, who often started their careers as trick riders and stunt men, have taught simulated falls with only the minimum risk to either humans or horses involved. It has been said that there were almost as many casualties in an early film version of *The Charge of the Light Brigade*, as in the actual event!

Sometimes horses and vehicles are borrowed for filming and television work from commercial firms and private individuals still using horse transport. Military and police horses may be pressed into service, especially on the Continent, while a well-known Yorkshire Brewery loaned several of its grey Shires for a farm sequence in a television version of the novel *South Riding*. Napoleon's Army on the field of Austerlitz and in the burning streets of Moscow, featured in King Vidor's *War and Peace*, was horsed by the Italian Cavalry, while the film known as *Waterloo* involved a then still unmechanised Russian Cavalry Brigade, the Royal Scots Greys in their famous charge 'Scotland For Ever' being played by a territorial unit attached to the Moscow Garrison, riding their own grey troop horses.

While horses are infrequently used on the stage, there are certain plays and operas in which they are indispensable. As a small boy the author was greatly thrilled to see an actual racehorse appear in a live production of 'The Arcadians'. Even today Brunhilda frequently mounts the funeral pyre on her faithful charger. Such animals are often house-trained, particularly the teams of Shetland ponies used in Christmas shows and pantomimes to draw the glass coach of the Fairy Queen. These are sometimes kept, as a temporary measure, not in the theatre, but at the stables of a nearby brewery or other commercial enterprise. When needed on stage they are conducted along the pavements, being harmless to pedestrians and voiding only in the gutters.

Bus harness to pole gear.

Above *Gerald Harper with two of the Tetley Shires on a television set* (Tetley's Breweries).

Left *Shooting sequences of* South Riding *with the Tetley Shires in the background* (Tetley's Breweries).

Above right *Shetlands used in pantomime stabled at Tetley's Brewery, Leeds* (Tetley's Breweries).

Right *Rehearsing for Christmas*

There are several teams of Shetlands in training for theatre work, usually all-greys, but sometimes piebalds or skewbalds, with long manes and tails. Some of the best known are owned by Phillip Gandey and Gandey's Circus, kept at his winter quarters near Sandbach in Cheshire, handy for towns of the industrial north and north midlands, where pantomime is still popular from Christmas to Easter. Those in Mr Gandey's keeping are small but well-proportioned animals of mainly mixed red and white colouring. There is one set of four, two sets of two, one red and white and one black and white. Ages range from three to approximately 25 years old, all commencing their show-business careers in the circus ring. They were all trained in advanced circus routines and learned to both accept and enjoy music, lights and the applause of large audiences. They have to be good natured and well-behaved as they frequently share the stage with large numbers of actors and dancers, including juveniles. All ponies are stallions or geldings. They are sent out on contract work with their own grooms, harness and sometimes a Cinderella coach and are always under strict supervision. No performing animals could be treated with greater kindness and consideration. In training sessions they frequently draw a wide number of miniature vehicles, specially designed for this purpose.

Promotions and advertising

Horses as trade marks and symbols are used by many firms, both on the hoardings, in the advertisement pages of magazines and for the promotional films of television and the cinema. Although not strictly involved in show business they have both publicity and entertainment value, drawing attention to a wide range of products or services, all of which have to be treated as minor dramatic productions. It would fill too much space to list the gamut of firms and products involved, ranging from scent and cider to machine tools and road rollers. Among the more outstanding, by any standards, are the White Horse Whisky advertisements with the slogan 'You can take a White Horse anywhere', stemming from the firm's use of a white horse symbol, since their occupation of the White Horse Cellars, Edinburgh, over three hundred years ago.

The Black Horse, in a rearing posture, has been a logo for Lloyds Bank over a number of years. It had previously belonged to early goldsmiths in the City of London, who were the precursors of the modern banking system in Britain. As far as can be traced a similar horse was used by a Master Humphrey Stokes, a goldsmith of Lombard Street, trading under this sign in 1666. Humphrey inherited the sign from his father Samuel, who founded the business even before the Civil Wars, although this is not officially recorded. There is a gap in the history of the rearing horse for several years, but it was later adopted by John Bland, another goldsmith of Lombard Street, who may have used the same offices. In 1749 Bland moved to another house of business but took the sign with him, eventually becoming established at 62 Lombard Street, where he remained for several decades. After a succession of new partners the Bland firm became known as Barnett Hoares, Hanbury and Lloyd. Lloyds Bank originated in Birmingham, emerging from a partnership between Sampson Lloyd and John

Right *The black horse logo of Lloyds Bank* (Lloyds Bank).

Below *'Hiron' filmed for Lloyds Bank in Ireland* (Lloyds Bank).

'Black Jack' filmed on Exmoor for Lloyds Bank (Lloyds Bank).

Taylor in 1765. The firm grew and prospered to become nationwide, extending its business to the City of London and merging with Barnett Hoares, Hanbury and Lloyd previously mentioned. The sign of the black horse remained through all these changes, becoming Lloyds own symbol in 1884, since the amalgamations of this period. A version of the sign, in modernised form, now hangs outside almost every branch in England, Wales and Scotland, also in many countries abroad as far apart as the United States, Russia and Japan. It has featured extensively in promotional and advertising campaigns, playing an increasingly important part in bringing the name of the firm before the public.

Up to 1972 use of the sign was in a fairly low key. During that year the bank changed its advertising agency to the firm of McCanns, who suggested a more lively use of the horse. For the first time a live horse was used on television commercials, a theme continuing from the early 1970s to the present day. The first horse was 'Hiron', who had been trained in a circus and performed many interesting movements, rearing-up and walking on his hind legs, as though by second nature, which was excellent for certain camera angles. When 'Hiron' died, some years ago, his place was taken by the current horse 'Black Jack' a privately owned hunter gelding, living in North Devon. This is a 19 year old animal greatly attached to its stable mate, a dun pony named 'Honey'. They are almost inseparable and follow each other about whenever possible. Many people wonder how the horse can be made to gallop about on the screen without any guidance or visible control, but the answer is simple. On a day of filming Honey is led on to the moors or a convenient open space, after which Black Jack is released and allowed to gallop after her, passing the cameras in search of his friend. 'Hiron' was filmed several times in Ireland, on location in bog and mountain. In order to film a bird's eye view a helicopter was used but came in a bit too close, causing the animal to bolt. It was many miles further on when the camera crew caught up with him, although by then he had calmed down and seemed none the worse for his fright.

Stage and mail coaches, as popular in the imagination of the romantic layman as Spanish galleons or knights in armour, have been frequently used in commercial promotions. They bring home the British sherry at Christmas time, while splashing with mire the would-be highwayman, who finds instant consolation in smoking his favourite brand of cigar. At one period, during the early 1960s, a road coach or private stage coach, crowded with Victorian-style passengers, toured the country making a plea for better roads and an extension of the motorways. The Norwich Union Insurance Company has long made use of such a vehicle, in which a record-making run was made between Bristol and London in 1984.

Colmans of Norwich, famous for their mustard and starch, among other products, own a magnificent horse-bus of the garden-seat type, that spent most of its early life on the streets of London. It was built about 1880 and carefully restored, almost reconstructed, in 1974–75 by the late Douglas Eley of Colchester. New wheels were made by the firm of Crofords. It operated a tourist coach service in the London area during the summer of 1975 hauled by a pair of grey Percherons, and also appeared in the London Harness Horse Parade in Regent's Park that year. Colmans acquired the vehicle in 1977, which now operates as a publicity gimmick, fitted-out with authentic signs in enamelled metal, advertising the firm's products. It makes frequent appearances in street parades and carnivals and at the opening of shops and stores where items prepared by Colmans are to be retailed. It has taken part in the inaugural procession of the

Campaign to improve the roads of Britain.

Above left *Garden-seat omnibus c1900*

Left *Horse Bus used to promote Colman's Mustard, 1984* (Colman's of Norwich).

Above *Horses owned by Mr Carl Boyde used to advertise Heinz Products. Driven by Mr B. Rolph* (Colin and Janet Fry).

Lord Mayor of Norwich and in the making of two films — *Murder by Decree* and the latest version of *The Thirty Nine Steps*. The bus is frequently loaned to the Suffolk Horse Society and is drawn by a pair of matching Suffolk Punches, owned by Cheryl Clark of Stoke-by-Nayland, near Colchester. It also appears for the Museum of East Anglian Life, making summer tours through the town of Stowmarket, laden with fare-paying passengers. Despite the possibility of cold or wet weather would-be passengers frequently scramble for a seat on top, near the driver, even though the upper deck is entirely unprotected. As on stage and mail coaches the place of honour is as near the driver as possible. Upwards of £100 per day is frequently collected in bus fares.

Chapter 5

Travellers by land and water

The open road

In the modern idiom a traveller is usually the representative of a large firm, touring the provinces to interest retailers in new lines of business. His occupation and mode of travel are very different from a normal concept of life on the open road and the bar of a commercial hotel no substitute for a camp fire beneath the stars. Yet only a few years ago there were thousands of so-called 'travellers' on the roads of Britain and throughout Europe, each with his horse-drawn vardo or living van, but more interested in telling fortunes or making clothes pegs than selling patent can-openers. They may have been attached to a travelling show or selling goods as market hucksters but were most likely to have been gypsies, also known as Romany-folk.

Large numbers of gypsies came to Britain and Western Europe from the Balkans and the Near East, during the 16th century. They are thought to have originated in Northern India or Central Asia but were essentially nomads, wandering at will in three continents. At one time so many claimed to have passed through or lived in Egypt, whatever the truth of the matter, that they were renamed people of Egypt, 'gyptians and eventually gypsies. Some settled, especially in countries that were less hostile to them, and became farming communities, but in parts of Northern Europe they were frequently harried and forced to 'move on', only camping in one place for a few days at a time, unless they could afford semi-permanent quarters for most of the winter months.

Those leading the travelling life only began to use living vans during the 1800s, and elaborate vardos were not in common use until the middle of the 19th century. By the 1860s they were widely adopted and remained in most families for over a hundred years. Before this gypsies had used tents carried on pack ponies and later on small carts. Gradually the tents became bow-topped structures over the cart and eventually were left fixed rather than being struck each time the gypsies moved on.

There were four or five main types of living van during their heyday. Those owned by wealthier horse-dealers were made entirely of matchboarding on a framework of strong wooden uprights or standards. These were the Reading and the ledge vans, the interiors fitted-out with elaborate bow-fronted furniture and spacious enough for tall men to stand upright. The bow tops and open lots were much smaller vans, the latter frequently constructed on the under-works of a

Above *Gipsy caravan, trap and horses under the elms at Pullox Hill, Bedfordshire in 1953* (Eric G. Meadows).

Below *Typical bow top caravan used by Romanies* (Hereford and Worcester County Museum).

Left *Rear view of a ledge van* (Hereford and Worcester County Museum).

Below *Bow top caravan* (Robert A. Smith).

Right *Reading van.*

delivery van or market wagon — especially after the Second World War when large numbers of such carts were replaced by motor vehicles. A few of these are still being made.

A procession of horse-drawn living vans crossing a village green or winding down a country lane was a familiar sight until the mid-1960s. From that period onwards many gypsies or travellers have taken to motor cars and trailer vans, joining traffic queues on motorways, side-by-side with towering juggernauts and family saloons; at last meeting on equal terms the purveyor of can-openers. Today only about six per cent still use horse-drawn vehicles, although many still trade in horses and make an annual appearance at Appleby Fair and other horse fairs throughout the country. Remaining vans are either open lots or bow tops, sometimes known as 'peg-knife wagons' as they can be made with a peg-knife and a few other hand-tools between dawn and sunset. Like the Red River carts of early settlers in western Canada, they may be roughly made but hang together for a long time.

Most of the early caravans which remain were made by specialist builders and are rich in carvings and gold leaf. The Reading type originated in the town of that name, made in a yard owned by the Dunton family. This was the Rolls Royce of living vans. The slightly narrower ledge van, its upper works overhanging the rear wheels, proved a close second in popularity. Many of these are now treated as curios and museum-pieces and seldom appear on the highways. Yet some owners

Left *Irish holiday caravan.*

Below right *Holiday caravans in the Black Mountains* (Welsh Horse Drawn Holidays).

Bottom right *On the road in the Wye Valley* (Welsh Horse Drawn Holidays).

of motorised vans, or older travellers hankering for 'the good old days', might take one on the roads for a short season, almost in the nature of a holiday. The scarcity of traditional vans is partly due to the fact that it was the custom in many gypsy families to burn the van on the death of its owner.

In certain parts of Britain, Ireland and Northern France, several firms now hire out horse-drawn living vans to holidaymakers and tourists. This was a trend that seems to have started in Southern Ireland during the early 1960s, where many of the traffic-free roads are still ideal for a wandering life, indeed there are still a fair number of tinkers and genuine gypsy families at large in this area. Most caravan holidays in Ireland are centred on the South-West and South. Those hiring in this part are advised to travel to Cork by sea or air. Arrangements having been made well in advance, the clients are met by private cars and taken to a base at Kilbrittan, from which a number of firms operate, this being six or seven miles from the popular holiday resort of Kinsale. Basic instructions and information sheets are available at the base camps, including selected routes for scenic interest and a list of country sites where the caravan may rest. The latter are usually fields owned by local farmers and hired-out at a cost of about £3 per night, which also covers grazing for the horse. Nearly all vans house four people in comfort and are equipped with bedding, mattresses, cooking utensils and other domestic requirements.

In England and Wales such holidays are available as far apart as the Isle of Wight, East Anglia and the Welsh Marches. In all cases the caravans are versions of the bow top, light and simple, but strongly made. They are fairly low, unlike the more traditional vans, allowing easy access and mounted on smooth running pneumatic tyres. Pneumatic tyres and disc wheels are easier to service, in modern times, than spoked wheels with steel tyres, and the average holidaymaker seems to dislike the rumble of metal on hard surfaces. A few places still hire the older vans, which are more picturesque if less practical, but available only on permanent sites or for short trips under supervision.

The oldest firm to organise self-hire caravans in Wales is Welsh Horse-Drawn Holidays based on Rhyd-y-Bont Farm, Talgarth, Powys. This is near the slopes of the Black Mountains and only a short distance from the Brecon Beacons or the beautiful Wye Valley. These are some of the most attractive parts of the country and also have the advantage of being provided with good roads and interesting places to visit, not least among which are hospitable wayside inns with fresh food, good beer and friendly gossip. On the day of arrival at Talgarth details may be obtained concerning routes and amenities. Previous experience with horses may be helpful but is not essential. The horses are peaceable and friendly, to be trusted with novices and young children. In the winter several of them may be used for heavier farm work and have even taken part in ploughing matches. Instruction is given in harnessing and how to handle the horse, with a supervised drive of two or three miles before setting out on the main ramble. Most hirings are for a week or a fortnight, commencing on Saturdays or Wednesdays. Caravans are two or three berth types, but whatever the size of the party a responsible adult over the age of

18 must be recognised as being in charge. Most items of cutlery and kitchenware are provided with the vans, as are blankets, buckets, kettles and frying pans. Pet dogs are welcomed by most firms in the hiring business but should be kept under control and tied-up at night. Cooking is by means of Calor Gas, supplied free to all hirers.

There are few better ways in which to spend a relaxed holiday away from it all. In the words of the Sunday Express correspondent reviewing Welsh Horse-Drawn Holidays — 'Sitting in the driving-seat, the air is sweet with the smell of the country ... the creak of the caravan behind and the music of the clinking harness in front.' Extra riding horses or ponies may be hired with the caravans from most firms.

The first pleasure caravan was designed by Dr Gordon Stables, an ex-Naval surgeon, author of adventure books for young people and a free lance journalist. On leaving the service for health reasons, he decided to wander about the countryside of Britain in a living van, drawn by two horses, mainly to lead a healthy, open-air life but also to gather material for his writings. He had already sampled the inconvenience of cycling, using pony carts and tramping on foot. As a man who liked his creature comforts a caravan was the only solution. This was not just a shelter at night but a place where he might write, sketch, print photographs and entertain his friends.

Setting out in the summer of 1886 he made a complete tour of England and Scotland, accompanied by a valet, a coachman, a cockatoo and a Newfoundland dog. On returning home he wrote a minor best-seller, known as 'The Cruise of the Land Yacht Wanderer', and also 'Leaves from the Log of a Gentleman Gypsy'. He had intended to start a club or association for caravanists, but this came a few years later, founded by other people. In the meanwhile the idea of caravan

Left *The first holiday caravan.*

Above right *An early photograph of the caravan 'Wanderer' on its travels. It was built by the Bristol Carriage and Waggon Works for Dr Stables* (The Caravan Club).

holidays began to catch-on and people of means were soon ordering or hiring horse-drawn caravans for their leisure use or early retirement, mainly inspired by the writings of Dr Gordon Stables.

A national Caravan Club was founded in June 1907, by ten men and a woman, all enthusiasts and owners, under the Chairmanship of J. Harris-Stone. This gentleman was a barrister and free-lance journalist. A friend of Gordon Stables, he was able to put many of the older man's ideas into practise. After the Great War the movement began to mechanise and horse-drawn caravans were soon outnumbered by motorised versions. The Wanderer had long gone into retirement and was eventually presented to the City of Bristol Transport and Industrial Museum by the Caravan Club, to whom it had been donated by Dr Stables' daughter. At Bristol it has been restored and refurbished, among many other interesting exhibits in the land transport section of the museum. This is appropriate as it was constructed in Bristol by the now defunct Bristol Carriage and Wagon Company. In 1982, on the 75th Anniversary of the founding of the Caravan Club, Wanderer again took the road, harnessed to willing horses, making a celebration trip between Bristol and London, ending outside the headquarters of the Club.

Left *Welsh Canal Cob.*

Below *Industrial canal.*

On the cut

Until the mid-1960s the canals and rivers of Britain formed watery highways for numerous cargo and passenger services. Many of the early boats and barges were horse-drawn, a fairly large number of horses, and also a few mules, remaining on Midland waterways up to the period of the Second World War.

Most of the narrow or boat canals, originally two-thirds of the inland waterways system, are now little used for commercial purposes, although supplying water to industry and providing cruiseways for pleasure boating in mechanically powered craft. In some places the towing paths have been neglected and are dangerous to horses but there are a few horse-drawn pleasure boats, mainly used for day trips and short outings in places of interest or outstanding natural beauty. For enjoying the peace and charm of the real countryside, few things are more relaxing than a horse-drawn boat trip, the motions of which are slow, gentle and almost noiseless. A slight swish of water and distant clop of hoofs, the rustle of reeds and the swaying of branches overhead are almost a therapy in themselves.

Several of these routes, and the boats and horses using them, have been described in a recent publication *The Horse on the Cut*. The following lines are merely to describe one or two of the more typical trip-movements, from information recently gleaned.

Frequent horse-drawn trips are now run over the Cromford Canal in Derbyshire, a section of which has been restored by a preservation society, responsible for both its working and upkeep. The author is indebted to Mr Simon Stokes, now General Manager of the Cromford Canal Society Limited (of which The Duke of Devonshire PC, MC is the President) for details relating to this concern. The Society was formed as a registered charity in 1971, becoming a company limited by guarantee in 1979, the voluntary work of members and enthusiasts augmented by two full-time employees and several others working under the conditions of temporary job schemes. The boat service began in 1977 and conveys passengers along restored sections of the waterway to see the historic Leawood Pumphouse, the latter returned to full working order and public viewing in 1980. Membership of the Society is open to all who wish to help with various aspects of running the canal.

There are two narrow boats, now provided with comfortable seating. One is the 'John Gray' which is a traditional open craft, able to seat sixty adults, while the 'Margaret A' seats thirty but is of modern design and has the advantage of an overall roof. Most trips leave Cromford Wharf at 2 pm and 4 pm on Saturdays, Sundays and Bank Holidays, from April to September. Journey time to and from Leawood is about two hours. During the week private charter services may be arranged in advance for mornings, afternoons or evenings. Bookings are not required for scheduled weekend trips. All enquiries regarding chartering and membership should be made to the Cromford Canal Society Limited, Old Mill Lane, Cromford, near Matlock, Derbyshire. A stamped, addressed envelope is requested for the return of up-to-date price lists and information sheets.

The Society now owns two horses, or rather ponies, replacing earlier horses which were hired or loaned for boatwork, as and when needed. The oldest of these

is now approaching 30 and mainly used for light work and short hauls. He is a gelding known as 'Strawberry' and worked for many years as a pit pony with the National Coal Board. When in draught he may wear either a neck or breast collar, and an open bridle without blinkers. Various straps and traces are worn with traditional bobbins that prevent the harness from chaffing the skin or fraying against hard objects. The harness was acquired at a sale but spare harness straps and a crupper or tail-piece have been specially made in the canal workshops, as have padded breast straps, from old belting, for breast harness.

In times of emergency or when an extra towing animal was needed a Hafflinger pony was frequently borrowed from the Duchess of Devonshire, who is President of the Hafflinger Breed Society. These splendid animals have been introduced from Austria, where they have been used for centuries in farm work, forestry and as military pack animals. They have a neat, attractive appearance with blond, flowing mane and tail, but are also tough and hard-working, able to survive the hardest winters in near artic conditions. It was purely coincidental, however, that when a new mare 'Tina', was acquired this should also have been a Hafflinger. 'Tina' was purchased in 1984 and is eight years old, expected to give many years of loyal service to the Society.

Left *Roving bridge which enabled the horse to cross the canal when the towing path changed sides.*
Below left *'Strawberry' hauling 'The John Gray' along the Cromford Canal. Note the use of a breast harness* (Cromford Canal Society).
Below *'Queenie', a canal horse working on the Kennet and Avon Canal* (Mary May).

For the technically minded, the towing rope used on both boats is 120 ft in length, hitched to the rear part of the harness by means of a swingletree, designed in the workshops. This is made of hard wood, straight in profile and round in section, incorporating snap-links for assembly and quick release. The colourful nose cans or bowls for feeding purposes are not used on this line, journeys being too short to make them worthwhile.

The ponies are stabled permanently on the wharf at Cromford, in adequate, purpose-built accommodation. Out of season they are looked after, visited and exercised by a number of volunteers. Both animals are attended at least twice daily throughout the year, including Christmas Day, Boxing Day and other public holidays.

In Berkshire a section of the Kennet and Avon Canal which, like the Cromford Canal, is undergoing restoration, may also be toured by horse boat. Here the arrangements are managed by a private firm, independent of the preservation society or British Waterways, run by Bob and Jenny Butler of the Kennet Horse-Drawn Boat Company. This firm has two craft, one now motorised and the other a traditional horse-drawn wide boat, painted with roses and castles in a style popular on the inland waterways for nearly 200 years. Bob and Jenny acquired the boats and one of the horses with the rest of the business in 1979.

The horse boat, known as the *Kennet Valley*, usually works from a wharf near Kintbury Lock, a few miles from Newbury. It contains a bar and seating accommodation for sixty adult passengers. Trips are popular with all types of people from school parties and works outings to social clubs and Women's Institutes. The Kennet Valley is highly photogenic and has appeared on several television programmes, and featured in an article 'The Canal Horse, Today and Yesterday' by Mary May, published in the March–April 1984 edition of *Horse and Driving*. The Earl of Snowdon has several times visited the boat and its horses, taking many photographs for an intended publication.

The boat is drawn alternately by 'Primrose' and 'Queenie', both mares of the small Shire type. 'Primrose' came with the business but 'Queenie' was purchased in 1982 from the Cotswold Farm Park where she had been engaged in cartage work. There is very little other traffic on this section of the restored waterway and learning the ropes was not a difficult task for either horse. In the past it was recognised that almost any type of horse could be used for towing boats or barges, although barges were usually heavier needing extra weight and strength. Starting the boat was the hardest part of the day's task, as once it began to move hauling become comparatively easy. Both 'Primrose' and 'Queenie' wear neck collars and harness decorated with colourful wooden bobbins. Their bridles are of the open type, worn without blinkers or nosebands. The all-nylon towing rope is 90 ft in length.

Another interesting horse-drawn trip boat works from the City of Chester, at the northern end of the Shropshire Union system. This is organised by the Chester Packet and Horse Boat Company, based on Tower Wharf, Whipcord Lane, Chester. It is the modern revival, over shortened distances, of a passenger boat service operating before the days of railways to link Mersey Ports with the

Above *Horse boats passing on the Llangollen Canal, 1981* (M. Brindley).

Right *Ridden boat horse about to leave Llangollen Wharf, 1981* (M. Brindley).

industrial Midlands. There is now only one boat and one horse, although a second horse is to be acquired in the near future. The boat is known as *Betelgeuse* and is licensed to carry fifty passengers. It has a galley, bar and small souvenir shop. It normally runs from near the city centre to the Trooper Inn at Christleton. Most trips leave Cow Lane Bridge at 2 pm, although evening and charter trips are also available for short distances. Some have the added attraction of an evening meal with live entertainers including instrumentalists, fire-eaters and pop-singers. The mare, 'Snowie', is a robust grey Shire type with plenty of feather or fetlock on her well-turned legs. She is very mild in disposition and a great favourite with young children.

Other horse-drawn trips are operated from Llangollen Wharf in North Wales, on the lower reaches of the Grand Union Canal at Berkhampsted, and the Caldon Canal in North Staffordshire, over a restored section of the Grand Western Canal in Devonshire and at the southern end of the Shropshire Union Canal between Market Drayton and Norbury. All craft have to be inspected annually by the Department of Trade and Industry (the former Board of Trade) and are licensed by British Waterways Board. Licensing is at the discretion of the Board and most trips are allowed only where the towing paths are in good condition and the use of horses does not clash with the needs of other traffic or commercial interests.

Chapter 6

On the range

Ancestors of the cowboy

The first cowboys as we understand the term today, strange as it may seem, were the herdsmen or gardiens of the Camargue in the South of France. Mounted Tartars and Mongol tribesmen have watched over flocks and herds since time immemorial, throughout the grazing lands of Central Asia, but these were always nomadic people, perpetually on the move and as much at home in the saddle as squatting in their felt tents or yurts. Gardiens, like western cowboys of the Americas, although sometimes sleeping out of doors, always return to a permanent home at the end of a particular work stint or cattle drive. They are, however, very similar to western cowboys in dress and general appearance, with narrow but flared trousers and broad-brimmed felt hats.

The home of the gardiens is the Rhone Delta, between two arms of the river, near their confluence with the Mediterranean. It is a strange land of rich pastures mingled with swamps, lagoons and sand-dunes. Since the Second World War large areas have been reclaimed for growing rice but there are still herds of semi-wild bulls and horses which have to be tended throughout the year. In dryer parts, where grazing is suitable, there are even large flocks of sheep. Gardiens, riding herd, are based on farms or ranches known as 'Mas,' which are mainly stone-built with walls thick enough to defy the severity of the changing seasons. This is not just man's work as, for centuries, women have ridden alongside their husbands and brothers, taking equal part in the drives and round-ups. Nearly all the people are natural horsemen, learning to ride as soon as they can walk and look after themselves.

Since Roman times and perhaps earlier, the local inhabitants have had a mystical regard for the small, yet agile and ferocious black bulls which were kept for sacrificial purposes in the cult of Mithras, with many deeply rooted religious and superstitious connotations. Today they are mainly bred to provide sport in non-lethal forms of bull-fighting, popular in all parts of Provence. This may be defined as a form of athletic contest, in which the bulls are teased and tested rather than slaughtered, the humans running far greater risks than the animals. One of the main acts is to snatch a rosette from the horns of a provoked and angry bull. An outstanding festival of the year accompanies the ferrade or sorting and branding of yearling cattle, often celebrated with formal displays of horsemanship.

French cowboy or gardien.

The horses of the Camargue, widely used in both herding and for ceremonial purposes, are nearly all greys and not much larger than fair-sized ponies. They are known as 'grignons' and are thought to have descended from a primeval race, as depicted in cave art, later mixed with African barbs brought to France and Spain in Moorish invasions. Although described by some as 'heavy and stupid looking' they are hardy, active and agile, at one time greatly in demand as cavalry remounts, especially for service in the colonies. One of their outstanding features is a long back having an extra bone in the spinal column. This may not make for a stylish conformation or suit the dressage and show-ring experts but it in no way hampers activity on the range or in the running of the bulls — known as Abrivado.

While the cattle are bred to provide both sport and meat, the gringnons are reared to horse the gardiens. In modern times tourists and seasonal visitors are encouraged to visit this part of France, where there are horses to ride and trails to follow, not unlike the dude ranches of the United States and Canada. Fighting bulls, both in Spain and Portugal, also in certain parts of Latin America, are still herded on large ranches or semi-open ranges. It was from the Spaniards that ranching and cattle herding were introduced to both North and South America. Many of the terms used in modern America such as rodeo, mustang and lasso are of Spanish origin, as is the type of saddle from which the western or cowboy saddle derives, the structure of which is ideal for roping cattle.

A cowboy's life

The cowboy rises at dawn and normally works a sixteen-hour day, if anyone's counting. He rides fairly upright in the saddle and holds the reins in one hand only, needing the other, usually the right hand, for a stock whip or lasso. The whip is also known as a bull-whip, especially in Canada. The western horse is guided through neck-reining, in which the pressure of a normally loose rein is tightened

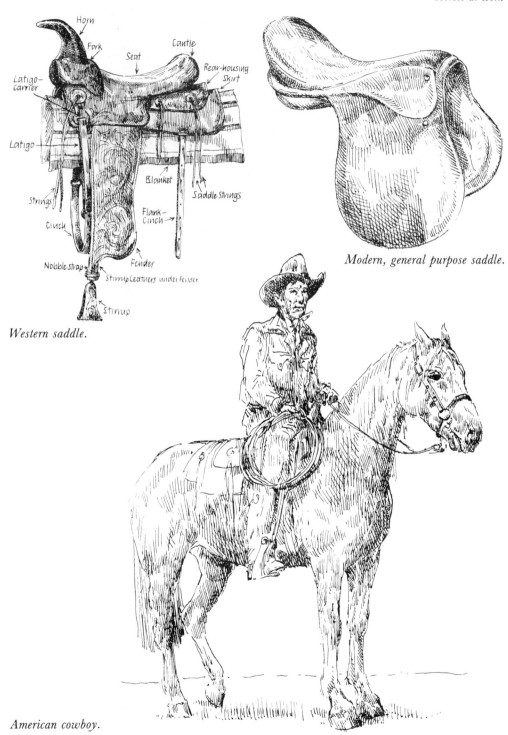

Horn

Fork

Seat

Cantle

Rear-housing
Skirt

Latigo-
Carrier

Latigo

Blanket

Strings

Saddle Strings

Cinch

Flank-
Cinch

Nobble Strap

Fender

Stirrup Leathers under Fender

Stirrup

Western saddle.

Modern, general purpose saddle.

American cowboy.

Cowboy in the Sawatch Mountains region of Colorado (The Bettmann Archive).

against the side of the neck. In response the mount automatically moves in the opposite direction or away from pressure. The general life-style is tough and down-to-earth, not exactly a pastoral idyll but having the clear advantages of good comradeship, usually good food and the good health that frequently accompanies outdoor living.

Unfortunately there are still cattle rustlers to be feared in many of the western states, reflecting the high prices to be paid for steak on and off the hoof. The modern cowboy has to be constantly on guard against such operators, especially in the proximity of through roads and metalled highways, and still goes armed with a six-shooter. These are not large-scale raids by picturesque bandits or indian braves, as seen in the films, with plenty of gun-play and galloping horses, although a man on horseback is frequently used. The modern rustlers work from a truck or trailer, these often disguised as something quite harmless. They draw in at the side of the road and a rearward flap is lowered from which the skilled roping artiste emerges, attempts being made to cut-off stray members of the herd, one or two of which may vanish into the night with scarcely a sound. There are no stops until reaching the big city and a convenient private abattoir.

Attempts have been made at different times and places to oust or at least augment the horse, using motor-bikes, helicopters and light aircraft. The faithful mustang, however, still proves the most effective and economical means of patrolling large herds. On some of the American ranches, often in high places and

Longhorn cattle on a large Texan ranch (The Bettman Archive).

foothills, where extensive use has been made of jeeps and motor-bikes, a few horses are also necessary to round-up strays, in places where wheels and even tracks are no match for good legs. In these circumstances horses are frequently conveyed to the location in trailer-boxes behind jeeps.

Strangely enough the man on horse or pony is widely accepted by herds of cattle and may sidle amongst them without much notice taken on either side. Yet once the cowboy dismounts, which he may be forced to do with any type of machine, he becomes an enemy and something to be feared or hated. Like the mounted policeman in a crowd the horse not only gives its rider unchallenged mobility but also serves as a point of vantage. In cutting-out and roping steers much of the work is actually done by the horse, who learns to anticipate not only the wishes of his rider but also the movements of the cattle. Most cow ponies are intelligent and sure-footed, able to gallop over uneven and rock-strewn ground in perfect safety. They are, however, a very mixed bunch, many descended from horses brought to the New World by the Spaniards, where the horse was for many centuries unknown. Others are morgans, quarter horses or American saddle-breds, frequently a mixture of all blood lines. Most of the above types have been bred in North America during the past two centuries proving ideal for a wide range of purposes, both ridden and driven. On some ranches, in recent years, a few pure bred Arabs have been used, with complete success, although they will probably prove too expensive for widespread use.

Dude ranches

People in the western states of North America have long been renowned for their hospitality and friendliness to strangers. Even during the middle of the last century wealthy tourists who came out to visit the range and sample life in the raw were entertained at the ranch house and able to see at first hand what was meant by roping, branding and even rustling, about which there has always been a steady flow of popular literature. It was only natural that these activities should be extended to serve the needs of paying guests after the First World War. Special ranches which catered for the needs of the tender-foot and eastern visitor became known as 'dude ranches' — the dude being a town dweller or man of leisure. These are still flourishing in large numbers and an important part of the tourist and holiday industry, although now virtually up-market holiday camps advertised in magazines and on television commercials. There is plenty of trail riding and elementary range-work under supervision, while some places even organise covered wagon treks through scrubland, to simulate adventures of the early pioneers. Not all dude ranches are in North America as, since the Second World War, several have opened in rural Britain and other European countries. Perhaps one of the best known was situated in the New Forest near Beaulieu, known as 'The Flying 'G' Ranch'. This catered for both holiday makers, staying long or short periods, and for morning trail-rides through forest clearings. Those taking part were expected to wear western clothes including traditional felt hats or stetsons and cowboy boots of tooled leather.

Rodeo and stampede

In the western states one of the most popular attractions for both tourists and genuine ranchers is the rodeo which has descended from the horse shows and riding displays of early Spanish settlers in what later became Texas and Mexico. This in its turn has spawned other minor industries and occupations, large numbers of ex-cowboys and would-be cattlemen following the rodeo circuit to compete for big prize money. There are championships involved in almost everything from roping and riding to the use of bull-whips, although perhaps staying on top of the bucking bull or bronco (wild horse) are the most popular. It may be noted that while some untamed and unbroken animals may be naturally dangerous, a great many in the corral or holding pens have been irritated by wearing an over-tight back cinch or rearward girth. This may be adjusted in such a way that even the most docile creatures are driven to a pitch of frenzy. They buck not to throw or destroy their rider but to rid themselves of the even greater discomfort of the cinch.

In Canada the equivalent of the rodeo is a stampede. The best known of these is the annual event at Calgary in Alberta, to which cattlemen, professional bronco-busters, tourists and fashionable drifters drive, fly or hitch-hike from all parts of the sub-continent. It is one of the great social and sporting events of North America to compare with the Winter Fair at Toronto and the Harrisburgh Horse Show. One of its most impressive features is the chuck wagon racing, said to be more thrilling and dangerous than Roman chariot racing. The chuck wagon was a vehicle used for taking food either to outlying field workers or to cowboys on the open range. Empty wagons, frequently escorted by outriders, often raced each other back to the ranch house, especially in pioneer days. This is now simulated in the form of an obstacle course, wagons having to be loaded by the outriders with assorted gear, including a clanging iron stove, after which they dash round the arena at full gallop, dodging casks and crates arranged as hazards, hopefully crossing the finishing line at the same time as their escorts.

Chapter 7

Remedial horsemanship

Riding horses has long been considered a healthy form of exercise and relaxation, one of the best ways to spend at least part of a country holiday. At one period doctors frequently recommended horse exercise, while even non-horsey people would snatch a brief hour in the saddle to stir up the liver. Those enjoying an ocean cruise or crossing the Atlantic in a five-star liner would even require mechanical horses to continue their daily jog in the ship's gymnasium.

The Ancient Greeks were known to have prescribed riding as an alleviation of mental or physical suffering and as a cure for certain ailments as early as the 5th century BC. People have thought along these lines, in many different countries over a number of years, but without serious or organised research. In the 1900s Dame Agnes Hunt, who founded a pioneer Orthopaedic Hospital at Oswestry in Shropshire, gave official encouragement to riding and caring for horses, in convalescence, as a means to recovery. This idea was further developed during the Great War, when sick and wounded soldiers were sometimes given therapy in riding classes, that helped to restore their equilibrium after the horrors of trench warfare.

Riding for the disabled

Inspiration for the present movement, known as 'Riding for the Disabled', stemmed from the heroic efforts of Madam Liz Hartel, a Danish polio victim, to overcome her physical disabilities and lead a normal life. Liz Hartel was struck down by what was then termed Infantile Paralysis during the 1940s but persevered with her riding activities to such an extent that she was able to enter the Olympic Games in 1952 and won a silver medal in the dressage events. Many people of all ages considered this a wonderful example and unspoken challenge, giving new hope to hundreds who had otherwise abandoned the idea of taking part in any form of sport or outdoor activities. While few of them would ever achieve such high standards or win prizes either for their country or themselves, it was as though a new dimension had been created. Apart from any physical benefits, the voluntary disciplines required in learning new skills and the pleasure of meeting others with like interests, were of incalculable value. Patients were lifted on to the back of a horse or pony and soon rode into another world, beyond the barriers of pain, inadequacy and sickly introspection.

Although the post-war movement may be said to have its origins in Scandinavia it was not long before its nationwide adoption in other European countries, especially in West Germany and Great Britain. During the late 1950s there were several groups active in different parts of the United Kingdom, nine of these joining together for mutual benefit in 1965. This was known as the 'Advisory Council on Riding for the Disabled', which became the 'Riding for the Disabled Association' in 1969. By the end of this year there were eighty groups in what is now a forward-looking and still expanding organisation.

The aim of the society is to help all types of disabled and handicdapped people, both adults and children, to regain confidence and enlarge their experience of life through contact with horses or ponies in ways that would be impossible if the only alternatives were inanimate or strictly mechanical forms of apparatus. To quote from a leaflet issued by the RDA — 'The term disability covers a wide range of handicaps which make it difficult to lead an ordinary life. We are conditioned to think of these handicaps as "physical" or "mental", but many people with a physical problem suffer psychologically and those who are mentally disturbed or retarded may also have physical disabilities.

'The object of the Riding for the Disabled Association is to give the opportunity of riding to any disabled person who might benefit in their general health and well-being. Disabilities with which the Association is familiar include cerebral palsy, spina bifida, disseminated sclerosis, muscular dystrophy, multiple injuries, limbless (including thalidomide), mental handicap, blindness and deafness.

'We also aim to help those aged 14 and over who express a desire to drive a pony or donkey-drawn vehicle. At present facilities are limited and priority is given to those physically prevented from riding.

'The RDA is finding that an increasing number of members of the medical and remedial professions do consider riding a helpful activity and a potential aid to rehabilitation in its widest meaning, particularly for many young adults who suddenly find themselves cut-off from their former pursuits by illness or accident.

'We recognise the wish of most disabled people not to be segregated or singled out for special treatment. We encourage participation where possible in Pony Club and Riding Club activities and stimulate interest in all aspects of the horse.'

Each local group has a chairman or organiser, with an instructor in overall charge of the riding activities. There is also a roster of helpers, and qualified therapists wherever possible, who are all voluntary workers. Helpers may be drawn from riding and pony clubs, the British Red Cross Society, the local police force, parents of children involved, older pupils and students at nearby schools or colleges and any responsible members of the community wishing to help. They are not all experienced horsemen but soon learn to interpret the wishes of the instructors, helping to create an atmosphere of confidence, security and companionship. Without this approach, although backed by concern and enthusiasm, much of the work would fail to be a success.

Horses and ponies may be owned by the group, lent by private owners or borrowed or hired from approved riding schools. The actual lessons, exercises and games take place in either open or covered schools, either privately or commercially owned. There are very few purpose-built centres but it is among the

Above *Riding lessons for disabled and handicapped children* (Riding for the Disabled Association).

Below *A young disabled rider makes friends with his pony* (Riding for the Disabled Association).

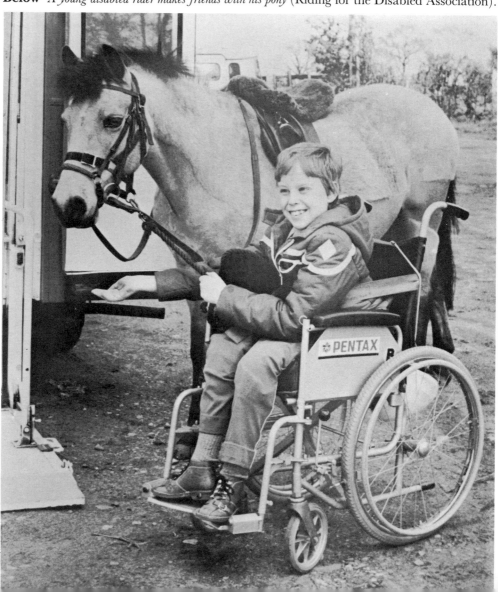

HRH Princess Anne meeting disabled riders (Riding for the Disabled Association).

aims of the society to create more of these, especially in towns and densely populated urban areas. While many come to the centres of their own initiative others are recommended for courses by their doctors, therapists, social workers or the heads of special schools and hospitals. To quote further from literature of the RDA 'We pay particular attention to safety. Every rider must have medical consent and the consent of parents if under the age of 18. Great stress is laid on the suitability of horses and ponies and safe equipment.'

The Patron of the society is HRH The Princess Anne GCVO who takes a keen personal interest in its activities. The President is Lavinia, Duchess of Norfolk, CBE, while the role of Vice-Presidents, each appointed for a three-year period, has many household names including Raymond Brooks-Ward MFH, Mrs Rachel Heyhoe-Flint MBE, Angela Rippon and Jimmy Saville OBE. The Director is Mr J. R. Moss MIPM, MBTM, to whom the author is indebted for permission to quote many facts on the preceding pages. According to figures in the annual report for 1983, there are now 18,647 riders of whom 14,131 are under the age of 18.

Horse therapy

Apart from the activities mentioned above there are other ways in which individuals either suffering or under treatment and restraint may be helped to recover by the use and presence of horses. At St Crispin's Hospital, Duston, Northampton, a Shire mare is frequently used on the hospital farm for general cartage work. This mainly includes feeding outlying stock in winter and delivering produce to the hospital kitchen, plus a limited amount of horse-hoeing in the surrounding market gardens. The extent of the work she does depends on the number of patients interested in and willing to work with horses. She has produced two foals, although unfortunately only one survived. These activities

are thought to have a beneficial effect on some patients, who take more interest in a working horse than they would in a lorry or tractor.

Perhaps the oldest continuing stud of Suffolk Punches, the heavy horse of East Anglia, is owned by HM Government. This is the Hollesley Bay Colony, administered by a branch of the Home Office, operating near Woodbridge, in Suffolk. It began life as the Colonial College and Farm Training Centre Limited, on part of a 1,800 acre estate, under the control of a Mr Robert Jackson. This was opened in 1887 for the purpose of training young men for emigration to the colonies and dominions, especially those wishing to be involved in farming and stud-work. Although the estate has changed hands several times, work at the stud has remained unbroken. The first stallion to stand at Hollesley Bay was recorded in the annals of the Breed Society as 'Hollesley Guardsman', acquired and registered in 1888.

From 1905 to 1938 the estate was administered by the Central Committee of the London Unemployment Fund. Its main work was to retrain unemployed industrial workers from the Greater London area for resettlement on small-holdings or in skilled country crafts. The scheme was abandoned shortly before the Second World War and Hollesley Bay taken over by the Police Commission (later the

Left *Suffolk Punches ready for ploughing.*

Right *A Suffolk in shafts.*

Prison Department of the Home Office) as part of the new borstal system for dealing with young offenders.

Today there are 1,400 acres of agricultural land, the remainder taken up by lawns, woods and playing fields. There are thriving herds of British Fresian cattle, flocks of Suffolk sheep and both Large White and Landrace sows in a modern pig-breeding unit. The Suffolk horse stud numbers about 25 animals and is mainly responsible for cartage and general estate work, also considered a supply centre for heavy horses needed in other borstal units. Horses are also sold to private buyers, both for daily work and show purposes.

Although a considerable part of the ploughing and cultivation on this self-supporting estate is now mechanised and the former number of horses slightly reduced, the Suffolk Punches still perform yeoman work in refuse collection, clearing scrap and salvage from workshops, also forage and dung carting. Most of the young horses are trained in all gears, as part of their breaking-in process. Suffolks are preferred, not only because they are the local heavy breed, but on account of a capacity for hard work and their even, kindly temperament.

Handling horses and general farm work are essential parts of the borstal training at Hollesley. The boys normally begin with stable routines such as grooming, cleaning harness and mucking-out. They progress to field work and the more responsible boys are soon given a post as carter with their own horse and cart to look after and keep in good trim. Those showing exceptional aptitude are trained for work with the stallions and show teams.

Work is long and hard, starting at six o'clock with two hours stable duties. Breakfast is at 8 am followed by field work and carting until noon. Horses are then returned to stables for a mid-day meal, but are out again by 1:30 pm, working in fields and lanes until 5 pm and the late afternoon feed. There is also an early evening session in the stables. While very few of the boys have prior knowledge of horses they quickly learn the techniques of grooming, harnessing, driving and feeding. There is always keen competition to advance a stage further and earn the privileges of trust. Working with heavy horses has an acknowledged value in character building and improving the sense of responsibility, while the breeding side of the stud is a worthwhile commercial proposition on its own account and unable to keep pace with the numerous demands for good working horses.

Chapter 8

Beside the seaside

Donkeys and carriage rides

Some of our earliest childhood memories may be based on seaside holidays. The pleasures of the first dip or building a sand castle closely rivalled by pony or donkey rides on the beach. After nearly two centuries of seaside holidays the ponies and donkeys are still there and, at many resorts local residents vie with holiday makers on hirelings for the joys of a canter over firm sand.

Phil Smith with one of his beach ponies at Seaburn, Sunderland. Phil's family have run a donkey and pony rides business on Sunderland's beaches all this century (Robert A. Smith).

Although a place to relax, the traditional English resort was also a venue to make a display of fashion and beauty. In this sense there was nothing more elegant, at certain hours of the day, especially in the late afternoon or early evening, than to enjoy a carriage drive along the promenade or in the marine park. Those who could not afford their own vehicles, in the days before horseless carriages, would engage a landau or Victoria, many of which plied for hire, with special ranks in a public square or near the end of the pier. These were single horse vehicles, usually open or with only a half-hood raised. The idea was to see and be seen, the factory and office workers at their annual wake, sampling the luxury of well-sprung and upholstered vehicles, riding in state and imagining, between pier and bandstand, that they were 'carriage folk'.

Most vehicles were driven from the box seat by a smart cabbie dressed as a coachman, often wearing top boots, white breeches and a frock coat. At Scarborough, however, there were a few so-called jockey-carriages, the horse between shafts ridden by a postilion with velvet jockey cap and waist-length shell jacket, the latter covered with buttons and braid. The postilion, known in Yorkshire as a 'jockey' which was the old English name for any type of horseman, must have had an uncomfortable ride, with his legs straddling the shafts, although no less than horse gunners during the first half of the 19th century when the wheel horses were in double shafts and the rear drivers had to contend with two pairs of thills (shafts) in parallel, almost rubbing against each other.

While there are still several seaside towns and inland resorts, both at home and abroad, where horse-drawn carriages are available to tourists, the majority in Britain are now to be seen on Blackpool promenade. This is one of the few towns in

Left *An evening cool-off at Seaburn, Sunderland* (Robert A. Smith).

Above *Square landau on the Prom.*

England where there are still water troughs used for their original purpose and cab ranks with rows of patient horses awaiting hire. One of the minor pleasures involved in visiting Blackpool, approached through the outer suburbs, is the occasional glimpse of a horse being groomed or put-to in the yard of an ordinary semi-detached or terraced house. The grooming of the horses and finish of the carriages is usually immaculate, great credit being due to the owners and drivers, especially when most of the vehicles have been in fairly constant use for over 70 years. A minor criticism might be that the general ensemble would appear even more attractive if drivers were as smartly turned-out as their landaus. Perhaps this is a reaction to general trends of informality — the modern pleasure-seeker in jeans and singlet might well flinch from the sight of smart liveries or even a well-pressed suit.

The horse-drawn landau is something of a novelty to visitors from urban areas where the horse has almost vanished, and is a great advertisement and publicity gimmick for what many regard as Britain's most popular seaside resort. It appears on picture post cards and in the brochures of the Corporation Tourist and Publicity Department, being as much a part of the local atmosphere as the famous tower and illuminations. If any of these attractions were to disappear Blackpool would cease to be a place of magic for both young and old. There are now 44 horse-drawn landaus licensed by the Corporation to ply for hire. One of the owners, a Mr B. Dolan, has featured on numerous post cards and runs his own open landau in conjunction with a riding school and carriage-hire service. Both horses and Victorian-style carriages or coaches may be hired for weddings and other special occasions needing a touch of style. Out of season, between late October and April, the horses are given a farm holiday, being in serious work for little more than half the year.

Nearly all Blackpool landaus are of the shallow canoe type, although there are also a few deeper, square-shaped vehicles. They usually have square candle lamps and are entered by means of a low step-iron on either side of the bodywork. During the holiday season traffic is always fairly heavy in the town and along the seafront, agog with family cars, taxis, buses and tourist coaches — so horse drivers are to be greatly admired for their skill in negotiating these hazards. Several take their pet dogs with them, which look most appealing when sharing the box seat. Most of the horses, in later years, seem to be built for comfort rather than speed or elegance, being a mixture of cobs and light vanners, some of the latter having a fair amount of feather or fetlock on their heels. The more spirited hackney-type is now an exception, although before the Second World War there were far more of what might be termed genuine carriage horses between the shafts. This may be a matter concerned with temperament and even problems of supply, although anyone with a genuine delight in horses is well-satisfied by the appearance of a healthy, clean and well-cared for animal, despite minor faults of breeding and conformation.

In 1981 the youngest holder of a hackney carriage licence was Gail Woodcock of Bridlington, on the north east coast. She was then aged 15 and still at school, working at weekends and during the summer holidays. The landau she drove is to be seen mainly along the sea front and belongs to her father. On her test drive one

Top *Landau waiting for hire on Blackpool promenade* (Peter Horsley).
Above *Rank for landaus near Blackpool Tower* (Peter Horsley).
Below *Holiday makers enjoying a landau ride along Blackpool promenade* (Peter Horsley).

of Gail's distinguished passengers was the Mayor of Bridlington, wearing his chain and robes of office. Both horse and carriage appear in splendid condition, a credit to its driver and the attractive resort where it operates.

Another landau often appears on Bridlington Promenade during the summer. It is owned by a local firm of coal merchants known as J. W. Nicholls and Company. They still use horses for street deliveries but during the slack season, when the weather is warmer and less fuel required by householders, one of the horses may appear in the shafts of a pleasure carriage. The same firm also provides horse-drawn vehicles for weddings and has been used for filming and television work.

The Douglas Horse Tramway

Another popular seaside attraction, this time on the Isle of Man, is the Douglas Horse Tramway which still uses 55 working horses. Douglas is the main town and port on the island and the system has been running for well over 100 years — its centenary having been celebrated on August 7 1976. It has survived not only the widespread electrification of mainland tramways, which eventually depended on power from overhead wires or underground cables, from the period of the Great War and earlier but also the general demise of trams in favour of the motor bus. Now, with the exception of the Blackpool trams and two show or museum lines, in Derbyshire and Devon respectively, the Douglas Horse Tramway is the only tram system in the whole of the British Isles.

It was founded by the railway and civil engineer Thomas Lightfoot (1814-93) who had been responsible for constructing the first Woodhead Tunnel through the Pennines. Although a Sheffield man he came to live in Douglas in about 1870, perhaps with the idea of making it a retirement home. Yet he could not remain inactive for long and suggested ideas for a street railway or tramway, the plans for which were drawn-up and lodged at the Rolls Office, Douglas, in 1875. There was considerable local support for the scheme, which was to be both a local amenity and tourist attraction. An Act of the Manx Parliament or Tynwald was promoted during the following summer and received the royal assent in the month of August. It was to be a 3 ft gauge line running from the pier or landing stage to Burnt Mill Hill, later known as Summer Hill. The maximum fare was to be 3d and at least six double journies had to be completed each week day. Only animal power could be used, without the Act coming under review. A single line track with passing loops was laid by the early summer of 1876, between the iron pier and Burnt Mill Lane, using 35 lb/yd rail. It had a centre treadway of tar and broken stone for the horses.

After a formal inspection by the Public Highway Surveyor the system was declared open, to be known as the Douglas Bay Tramway Company. Two double-decker cars, each drawn by a pair of sturdy horses, had been ordered from the Starbuck Car and Wagon Company of Birkenhead, makers of some of the earliest and most reliable tram or street cars in history.

In January 1877 an extension of the line was opened to the new Victoria Pier. Three tram cars were now in use with a stud of 15 horses, stabled on land owned

Douglas horse tram.

by Lightfoot at Burnt Mill, almost in his backyard, a former walled garden converted for use as a car depot.

By 1882 Lightfoot became involved in other enterprises, including the building of shops, business offices and a holiday hotel. At this stage he may have over-reached himself and been in need of hard cash, for he sold his interest in the 'trams' to a consortium of three businessmen who formed a new company known as The Isle of Man Tramway Limited. The number of passing loops were soon increased and regularity of service much improved. There were, by this time, seven double-deckers and one single-decker. The last double-decker was purchased in 1884 and two new single-deckers, with seating on the crosswise or toast rack plan, were introduced in 1885, each drawn by a single horse. In 1887 double tracks were opened over part of the route, and were extended in 1891. By that time 26 cars were in service and passenger-carrying had increased to 628,842 per year, rising to 803,144 a year later.

From 1894 the system was acquired by the Douglas and Laxey Coast Electric Tramway Company for £38,000. With the opening of a new line to Laxey, for electric workings only, the name was further changed to the Isle of Man

Tramways and Electric Power Company Limited. The year 1897 was a time of further records with one and a half million passengers carried. Throughout this period a good draught horse could be kept for as little as 9/3d per week. Double tracks were now laid throughout, eliminating an earlier bottleneck of single track between the Castle Terrace and Loch Promenade.

In February 1900 Dumbell's Bank failed and the Tramway Company was deeply involved in the ensuing crash. Because of this the tramways and the electric power company were forced into liquidation. The horse-drawn lines and a short cable-hauled system were acquired by Douglas Corporation, while the electric railway was sold to a syndicate which became known as The Manx Electric Railway Limited. At various intervals there was talk of complete electrification but this was resisted for several different reasons, mostly based on a mixture of shrewdness and sentiment as horse-worked tramways were becoming a rarity on the mainland and considered in the nature of a nostalgia trip. There was, however, a considerable slump during the First World War, when fewer holiday makers and day trippers came to the island and much of the interior was occupied by prisoner-of-war and safe internment camps. Motor buses, still something of a novelty on the island, began to challenge street cars of all types and from 1927 it was decided to run the service on a seasonal basis only.

During the Second World War there was total closure. Hotels and holiday flats along the front at Douglas were requisitioned for the internment of aliens and political dissidents, while barricades or barbed-wire entanglements covered running tracks, both to repel would-be invaders and make confinement more secure for the internees. A greatly restricted service was opened in March 1946, relying on 42 horses newly imported from contacts in Northern Ireland. This soon

Douglas horse tram c1950 (Douglas Corporation).

Parade of tram horses in 1956 on the 80th anniversary of the Douglas Horse Tramway (Douglas Corporation).

began to show a healthy profit and with the holiday boom of the following year it was decided to fully reinstate and extend the service, relaying the tracks throughout. The tramway service now operated with single-decker cars only, each car hauled by a single horse; one double-decker remaining on a siding at the depot was seldom, if ever, used. In 1955 the double-decker was refurbished, given a new coat of paint and presented to the Museum of British Transport in London.

In 1956 the line celebrated its 80th Anniversary, running an average of 26 trams per day and carrying upwards of 30,000 passengers. On the actual day there was a parade and drive past of all the men and horses employed on the line, from the depot to Victoria Pier. This was watched and applauded by the Lieutenant Governor and numerous distinguished guests, including the granddaughter of the founder and Pat Smythe, the international show-jumping celebrity. Later in the day, after a celebration lunch, Pat Smythe drove tram No 40 on a special trip to Derby Castle, the promenade lined four-deep with cheering holiday-makers.

During the early 1960s the pattern of British holidays was beginning to change although figures in such areas tend to fluctuate through whims of fashion. The closure of the Douglas to Fleetwood steamer service certainly did not help matters, although the horse tramway continued to flourish, but with increased fares. In 1964 HM The Queen Mother visited the island and graciously rode on car No 44, hauled by 'Winston', one of the oldest but most reliable horses in the stud. Princess Margaret and Lord Snowdon also visited the system in July 1965 and the Duke of Edinburgh came in 1970. Figures had been dropping during the past few years, but by 1966 they were shooting up again, with a rise to over one million in 1974. By 1972 the number of horses had increased to 70 with services of

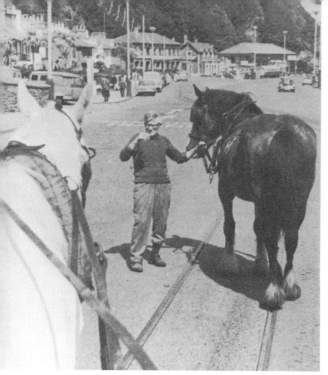

Above left *Changing horses at the Victoria terminus of the Douglas Horse Tramway* (Douglas Corporation).

Above right *Tram horse, Douglas, Isle of Man.*

Below *Passing the time of day with a Douglas tram horse* (Douglas Corporation).

1½ minute intervals at peak periods during the height of the season. This was also the year of an official royal visit, when at 10 am on August 2 Her Majesty Queen Elizabeth II, accompanied by HRH The Duke of Edinburgh, disembarked from the Royal Yacht *Britannia* at Victoria Pier and made her way to the terminus of the horse tramway. Two specially decorated cars were at the disposal of the royal party, the Queen riding in the first of these, car No 44 in which her mother had travelled eight years earlier. This was hauled by an 11 year old roan mare named 'Pearl' and driven by the former stable foreman J. Moughtin, who retired that year. The car conductor, acting as host, was Jack Corris, later promoted to traffic inspector. The short drive along the front, between cheering throngs, was to the steps of the Sefton Hotel, where a civic reception and lunch had been planned.

From 1974 it was decided to breed horses to serve the line on farmland owned or leased by the Corporation. The price of suitable horses had risen dramatically, by at least 100 per cent, and due to the troubles in Northern Ireland there were restrictions on this source of supply. During that year there were 60 horses and one foal at the stud, and six mares were known to be in foal. The first foal was born on August 31, its sire being a stallion from Balnahowe Farm, near Douglas.

Although motor buses are also run by the Corporation Authorities, with high fuel and operational costs, these are now subsidised by the horse trams.

The stables of the tramway system are situated near the sea front, next to the Crescent Hotel, on land acquired by Thomas Lightfoot in 1887. This area is known as the 'Queen's Promenade'. Permission for visitors and holiday makers to view the stables and stud may be granted after a courtesy visit or formal application to the transport offices at Derby Castle terminus. The stable block is fronted by a row of charming terraced houses, rooms of which are used by the tramways and stable staff. Minor harness repairs are also undertaken in one of the downstairs rooms. Major repairs and the making of new items are now the responsibility of a large firm of commercial saddlers in the City of Glasgow.

Large double doors next to the Crescent Hotel open into what is known as the front yard. To the right other doors lead into five stable-rooms, all in constant use during the summer season. Each stall is high and spacious, shuttered from the neighbouring stalls by barriers of solid, unpainted woodwork. The name of the occupant is chalked above the stall and its neck collar hung from a wooden peg at the side. Horses are tethered by a running line that allows them to stand or lie down at will when off duty. There is a feeding trough or manger across the far end of each stall with a hay rack in one corner and a fresh water supply in the other. The floors are covered with a good bed of straw, which is naturally changed every day. Upper stable-rooms are reached by means of gradually sloping ramps, two floors being used, on one of which there are two fully enclosed boxes. Behind the stable block is a large blacksmith's shop and a rearward yard, enclosed by tall cliffs.

Five men are employed in the stables during the winter months, under the direct control of the Transport Manager. During the summer season there are approximately 35 men in stables. Although the tramways now breed their own horses, these were formerly bought at the age of six, mostly unbroken. A good horse is likely to give 16 years' service to the line. Training for horses takes about six to eight weeks, after the usual 'young horse' schooling and breaking. There are frequent early morning sessions for this purpose with empty vehicles, when there is very little other traffic about and conditions are fairly quiet. Most horses are well-accustomed to routine long before the end of their first season. Some of the older and more reliable animals work an evening shift at the height of the season, and seem well used to flashing lights of traffic and overhead illuminations. The men operating or driving the cars need about 100 hours training.

Cars banned

On the holiday island of Sark in the English Channel Islands, no motor vehicles are allowed, apart from a number of farm tractors. Cars, lorries and motor buses were made taboo by feudal decree of a former Dame of Sark, by whom the island was both owned and governed. Incoming tourists from Jersey and the mainland are met on the quay by Victoria and wagonette that vie with each other in the smartness of their turn-out and paintwork. Many of the carriages or Victorias are of a square type once popular in all parts of the Channel Isles and known as 'chairs'. A number of more commercial-looking vehicles known as 'vans' also appear, capable of taking 12 adult persons per trip.

Although much of the regular farmwork is now done by tractors, during some of the few bad winters when fields were muddy and difficult to work, horses are often preferred, called into service where tractors are frequently bogged-down. Most horses are worked throughout the week between shafts and given a day of rest on Sundays. The only exception is when an elderly person or invalid needs to be driven to church or to the harbour. A horse-drawn tour of the island is a popular diversion which lasts, with stops at cafés and hotels for refreshment, about three hours. There are also romantic evening trips by candle-lamp and moonlight. During the first week in September there is an official Sark Horse Show and Gala, with events for driving and turn-outs but also a flat race under saddle known as the 'Sark Derby', most of the horses taking part having also appeared between shafts earlier in the week.

It was forecast that when the Dame of Sark died, restrictions would be lifted in a rush to mechanise, but this has not proved the case. Many visitors and holiday makers are delighted to be free of private motoring which, whatever its merits on the mainland, would be totally out of place on so small and peaceful an island. Fortunately many islanders share this view and the internal combustion engine may be held at bay for many years to come.

Since 1968 there had been a licensing of horse drivers and new drivers on the island have to take a strict test. Only three attempts are allowed — pass or fail. Would-be drivers have to be resident in Sark for at least ten days before attempting the test. During this time they are expected to learn something of the history and geography of the island in order to point out places of interest and answer the questions of tourists. Some drivers come from the mainland or other islands and merely stay for the holiday season, between early April and October.

Chapter 9

On the farm

Mechanisation versus the horse

During the 1930s there was a widespread urge to mechanise, especially on the farm, the internal combustion engine having an almost compulsive fascination for the increasing number of farmers either outfacing bankruptcy or exchanging their 'way of life' for big business methods. Lease-lend from America during the Second World War encouraged the purchase of even more tractors so that by the late 1950s the horse had almost disappeared from the land. It was a gloomy enough prospect not only for the sentimentalist and enthusiast but also for deeper thinking realists. Yet eventually the cost and scarcity of both natural and synthetic fuels caused some of the more discerning to rethink their attitudes. From the late 1960s a reaction had begun to set in and while exponents of what might be described as 'total farming' still held sway, at least their modes and methods were under scrutiny. There was almost an outcry in certain quarters for reserve forces

Bringing home a sick lamb on a Welsh hill farm.

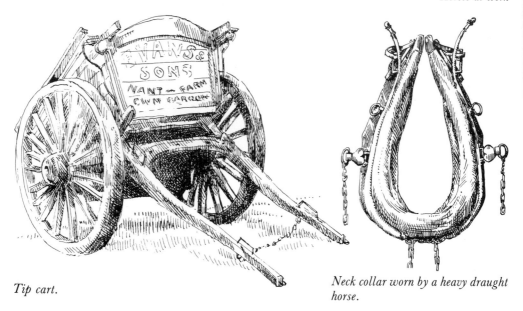

Tip cart.

Neck collar worn by a heavy draught horse.

and alternative methods to meet unforseen future needs, while in the short term thinking men wondered if it was necessary to use a machine representing many horse power and costing thousands of pounds to do the work of a single horse. Strangely enough it was in America that a need for change was first recognised. Although among the leading nations to pioneer mechanised farming the United States was also the first to question and reject over-mechanisation. Today the number of horses and mules on American soil has greatly increased, not even taking into account the number of religious communities, such as the Amish Folk and Mennonites, who depend on horses both for farming and transportation.

There are several self-dependent religious sects in North America, of which the two mentioned above are perhaps the most typical. Although certain Amish people have now come to terms with motor vehicles as a means of communication (the Auto-Amish), many still drive themselves in specially designed buggies and road wagons, while all the essential farm work is done by horses, mules or oxen. Refugees from intolerance in other lands, they settled in the eastern states of America during the late 18th and early 19th centuries, continuing to work and act in the same way as their ancestors — refusing to accept modern inventions as a token of their gratitude for deliverance. Despite predictions to the contrary their farming enterprise has prospered, maintaining a higher level of commercial success than the alternate boom and slump of fully-mechanised farming, with its dependence on high finance, political intervention and rising fuel costs.

There are many jobs about the farm that are ideally suited to real horse power, especially carting and feeding out-lying stock. Horses are also useful in orchards and market gardens, particularly for cultivating between planted trees. On hill farms, where tractors frequently over-turn on steep slopes, the horse and cart or wheel-less drag are far better than either wheeled or caterpillar tracked tractors,

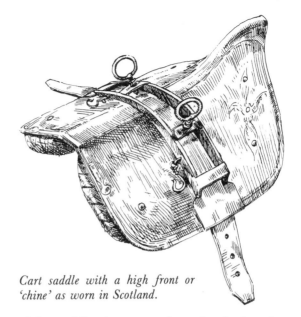

Bridle worn by a heavy draught horse.

Cart saddle with a high front or 'chine' as worn in Scotland.

due to the distribution of excessive weight and fixed centres of gravity. In farming areas with heavy soil which are subject to water-logged conditions, the mechanised farmer is often at a serious disadvantage, especially in winter, and may be forced to hire horses from other concerns or waste a considerable amount of the time and money which mechanisation was expected to save. Hauling timber on hillsides is a further example of the horse proving irreplaceable, and many others could be mentioned. In some cases, however, the exponents of mechanisation are too prejudiced to recognise, much less admit, their limitations.

There is still room for horses in certain types of daily work and on particular locations, yet one of the difficulties is finding and training a new generation of horsemen to look after their equine charges. Although plenty of people come forward when jobs with horses are advertised the glamour sometimes outweighs the necessary enthusiasm. Large commercial stables in towns may be able to stagger hours to cover holidays or weekend duties, but this is not always possible on a farm, especially the smaller holdings. To make the reinstatement of horses meaningful those concerned must have character, patience and sheer dedication. This applies not only to agriculture but to the mounted trooper, police officer and commercial coachman, in fact to all who opt for a permanent career with horses.

Fortunately there have been a fair number of recognised courses in recent years, especially at farm centres, where people keen to learn more about horses are initiated into skills concerning them, if only at an elementary level. A young person intending to spend a whole career with horses would almost certainly benefit from a minimum period of service in a branch of the army still using them. One of the courses mentioned above was run by the University of Nottingham Department of Education for Adults combined with the Worker's Educational Association, at the Horncastle Residential College, Lincolnshire. This included

Left *Using a reaper-binder in the 1980s* (Devon Shire Horse Centre).

Below left *A pair of Clydesdale plough horses* (E.J. Anderton).

Right *Ardennes horse.*

both lectures and practical demonstrations, and was entitled 'The Horse on the Farm'. Those taking part represented not only the farming community but people from many different walks of life including housewives, and representatives of the Church and the Royal Air Force.

From the mid-1970s courses have been held, mainly concerning horses in agriculture and forestry, on the Dorset farm of Charley Pinney, backed by the Agricultural Training Board. The first stage of these concerned basic harnessing, leading to handling, driving and stable management. On the first day of three day courses students learnt how to prepare a horse for daily work, using shafts, pole gear and traces. Both two and four wheeled vehicles or implements were driven round obstacle courses, graduating to work with wheel-less drags, harrows and rollers. It is now the policy of the ATB to encourage the formation of suitable schemes and courses in all parts of the country. Instructors are drawn from the ranks of working farmers and experienced horsemen, who are themselves given a short course as would-be teachers at the regional headquarters of the Board. A passed instructor is awarded an agreed instruction rate and grants to cover the use of horses, land and equipment. It may be noted that Mr Pinney, working over 250 acres at the Home Farm, Bettiscombe, near Bridport, is a keen supporter of the Ardennes breed of horse, which he considers ideal for modern agriculture. Most of his horses are worked in open bridles, without blinkers or eye shields. He is personally responsible for designing and constructing several types of vehicles and implements for everyday use, including a patent hitch cart developed on the articulated principle.

In March 1979 there was an important Shire Horse Seminar held at the National Agricultural Centre, Stoneleigh, Warwickshire. This was attended by

Above *Shire gelding to a seed drill, sowing seed corn on a Hampshire farm* (Colin and Janet Fry).

Above right *Shire gelding harrowing a seed bed on a Berkshire farm* (Colin and Janet Fry).

Right *Shire mare working winding gear and a John Willis Type 625 Elevator built in 1880* (Colin and Janet Fry).

large numbers of horse-owners, both professionals and laymen, covering practical demonstrations and lectures by several leading experts. Among those to speak was Mr David Kay of Daniel Thwaite's Brewery, Blackburn, a leading figure in the heavy horse world of Lancashire and the north west.

While it may be hoped that the gallant Shires and Clydesdales will always have their active supporters, it is now the turn of the smaller breeds to prove their worth. These latter include several types imported, during recent years, from Belgium, France, Austria and other countries. They were almost unknown on this side of the English Channel before the Second World War but have now gained a considerable following. For marginal work on average or mixed farms the Shire, although an excellent waggoner and show horse, tends to be over-sized for many of the jobs in hand. He is harder to handle and requires much better and more expensive feeding for the amount of work done, than smaller horses. The French Ardennes breed is a case in point being strong, docile and active in a height range between 14.2 and 16 hands high. For short haul carting even the ponylike

Left *Cart saddle as used on farms in Herefordshire and Worcestershire.*

Right *Field roller.*

Below right *Harvest wagon.*

Bottom right *Pair-horse mower.*

Hafflinger has been recommended, while the Welsh Cob has long been one of the most versatile equine creatures both ridden and between shafts. All these are mountain breeds and, like most of their kind, nimble, willing and sure-footed. Compared with some of the modern draught giants, gentle or otherwise, the smaller types have been bred and trained for real work, which makes a considerable difference to character and temperament.

Having praised the smaller breeds it must be acknowledged that, on their own ground with heavier loads, the Shire, Clydesdale, Suffolk Punch and Percheron are hard to beat. They each have their good points and characteristics, while many Englishmen have a deeply felt, almost sentimental leaning towards Shires, which seem so much a part of their history and tradition. It is to be hoped, however, that a craze for size and fashionable appearance does not turn an honest breed into mere show animals, important as showing may be.

One of the original homes of the Shire horse, descended, as many now claim from the Great Horse (or War Horse) of England, is the Lincolnshire Fens. Here, even with so many dykes and drains, the level ground frequently becomes tacky and hard to work. Some farms and holdings in this part are very large, well over the 1,000 acre mark, an important main crop being potatoes. One of the great potato and root farms is at Morton Fen, Bourne, where the daily routine is shared between horses and tractors. In the early 1930s there were 36 'heavies', but the number is now reduced by more than half, there being 15 horses and 15 tractors. During certain wet seasons of the late 1970s, when rain was fairly continuous throughout the autumn months, tractors and the heavier types of vehicles or machinery were unable to work in the deep mud. Without horses and the traditional tumbrils or two-wheeled farm carts, it would have been impossible to save the harvest. Every year both corn and potatoes are carried by means of willing Shires, Suffolks and Percherons — there being a few of each type. While most farmers in this area use combines for their corn crops, at Engine Farm, Morton Fen, good quality straw is still a saleable item and cut by means of tractor-drawn binders. The average reaper-binder is a heavy, cumbersome affair and few

now expect these to be horse-drawn. Sheaves dropped by the binder are gathered into neat piles or stooks where they dry-out before lifting, taken to the stack-yard or storage area in carts drawn by two horses — usually a shaft horse and chain horse in tandem. Straw is seldom much use from a combine harvester, being torn, battered and ragged, unsuitable for thatching or any worthwhile purpose. At Engine Farm it is mainly reserved for the makers of large steel pipes, sold at £70 to £80 per ton for lining joints between them, for which no other material, not even artificial straw, is equally suitable.

In the potato fields horses work to the command of human voices and are very popular with most pickers and piece-workers. The smoke, fumes and throb of

Left *Percheron.*

Below left *Flemish horse (Belgian).*

Below *Decorated Shire.*

Right *Carting at Devon Shire Horse Centre* (Devon Shire Horse Centre).

machinery scarcely makes for more efficient working conditions and there is always a feeling of comradeship between man and beast. Traditional carts are used with steel-tyred wheels rather than pneumatics. From the design view point steel rims not only look more attractive and workmanlike but are also more efficient. Rubber cart tyres with treads working on farmland, especially in rainy weather, are always picking up lumps of mud which gradually mould into skids over which the carter and horse have only the minimum control. There is very little sentiment about the workings of such places as Engine Farm, both horses and tractors have their separate duties and are complementary to each other. In all parts of the world people with sense and judgement are, or should be, working on the same lines, able to recognise that horses and machines do not replace each other — except in the glib talk of sales promotions — but work more efficiently in close harmony.

One of the first men in Britain to support a revival of the heavy horse in agriculture has been Geoff Morton, formerly an officer in the Merchant Navy but

Above *Clydesdale gelding doing his first work in harness by pulling a sleeper* (Colin and Janet Fry).

Below *Using tedders to turn the hay* (Devon Shire Horse Centre).

from a traditional farming background, who runs Hasholme Carr Farm, Holm-upon-Spalding Moor, in what was formerly the East Riding of Yorkshire. He works the land entirely by real horse power but also hires out teams for filming, television work, carnivals and general promotions. There is also a wide range of vehicles and working implements available, all attended by experienced farm workers and horsemen. The advice of Geoff Morton to all would-be heavy horse users is to invest in breeding stock or brood mares and breed for future requirements. From the economic view-point, buying a mature horse of quality as and when needed is the most expensive way out of the problem. One of the great disadvantages of the tractor is that it cannot reproduce itself.

It has been claimed by some experts, in recent years, that numbers of horses would have lasted much longer in the main stream of British agriculture, if they had been used in larger teams. This idea may seem contrary to other modes of thought and is essentially a point of view, most people seeing a heavy horse revival mainly in terms of single cartage work and isolated movements. Yet the multi-furrowed gang plough drawn by teams of six or more animals would seem to be the only possible challenge to the supremacy of the tractor, in this area of cultivation. British farmers, with much smaller fields than those to be found in American and colonial farming, have been reluctant to use hitches of more than one or two horses at a time. North American farmers made far more economical use of large teams and riding implements because they were often short of skilled labour (especially good horsemen), although less restricted by acreage. With so many hedges grubbed out and fences or walls removed during the post war period, and also loss of man-power through over-mechanisation and a townward drift, the American approach might now begin to make sense in rural Britain. With an eight horse hitch a combination of five chain harrows and four rollers may be worked together.

By the 1950s the supply and production of horse-drawn farm machinery in Britain came to a sudden halt, so that only second hand implements were available. Spare parts are still almost non-existent and many of the machines or implements in regular use are over 40 years old. Fortunately some horse-drawn machinery is still available from sources in North America and Eastern Europe, especially Poland, while a few small or individual manufacturers are now attempting to meet specific needs, although still on a small scale. Such concerns as the Cotswold Farm Park have even invented and introduced new types of machinery for horses. One of their latest and most efficient appliances is a new type of manure or muck spreader. One of the areas hardest hit by shortages is match ploughing, which although becoming a competition of increasing popularity, may soon be hampered by a universal shortage of the right plough shares.

Forestry

Although horses are unlikely to replace tractors in certain land work there is always a place for them in timber extraction. On the wooded slopes of both new and traditional British forests the horse makes good economic sense. Horses are accepted for their flexibility, especially in the work of selective thinning. The

Wood clearance using a Clydesdale (Clydesdale Horse Society).

alternatives are to make broad tractor ways with line thinning, which equally destroys good trees and those of inferior quality, while increasing the danger of unwanted wind blows. Horses can operate over much steeper and more difficult terrain than most tractors and even where specialised machines are used it is far from economical to bring them long distances for occasional work in odd corners. To overwork the forest areas with heavy machinery, as in some arable farming, may lead to hardening or compacting of the soil also the destruction of necessary drainage runnels and access tracks, the latter frequently churned to morass, while roots are destroyed and trunks or boles badly scarred in ways that may be avoided by horse teams. The pressure of hoofs in such circumstances even helps to regenerate the upper strata or soil-mantle, whereas heavy wheels and tracks only destroy the top soil.

It is essential that horses are well-trained and worked by competent horsemen. Young or inexperienced animals may tangle themselves in their gear and traces or bolt at the unexpected noise made by chain-saws and other mechanical appliances. Special trace gear is worn for taking out felled trees or 'timber snigging', with chains round each log hooked to a swinglebar and passing to the neck collar, through the backband and upper body harness.

There is still a considerable amount of horse-worked timber hauling in Central Europe and Scandinavia. A work study department of the British Forestry Commission recommended the introduction of Continental-type gears and several sets of purpose-designed harness were imported, but not widely appreciated or accepted by British forestry workers.

Ploughing matches

Oddly enough, since the post-war decline of farm horses, there has been a revived interest in ploughing matches in all parts of Britain. This must be one of many reactions against over-mechanisation but is also a test of skill and craft, to be admired for its own sake. The county or area ploughing match is also an important social occasion in the countryman's diary, with classes for both horse and tractor ploughs, also for hedging, hurdle-making and other skills — a meeting place for those with many like interests. Horse ploughing is often the main attraction, which may be slower but of a higher quality and greater depth of furrow than mechanical methods. The finest horse ploughing is also known as 'high cut work'.

At most ploughing matches there are both 'high cut' and 'general' classes. As might be expected, 'high cut' is neater, smoother and more regular. The high or crested cut may be from 6 in to $7\frac{1}{2}$ in wide, the upper two sides of each furrow being of near equal length. 'General' work is performed with a semi-digger plough of a type introduced during the late 19th century and developed from the digger

Clydesdales at a ploughing match (E. J. Anderton).

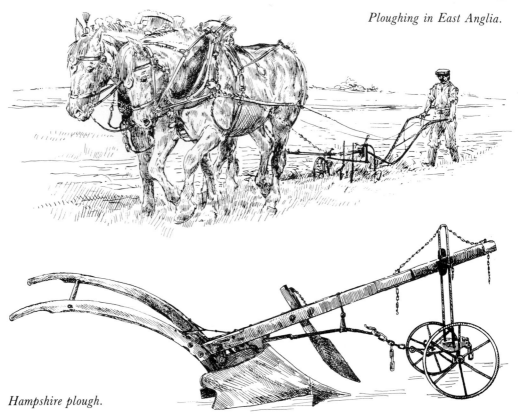

Ploughing in East Anglia.

Hampshire plough.

plough of 1885. Digger or digging ploughs had a short mouldboard, for horizontal cut, with a greater curve of the board than on other types. This was suitable for light to medium soils but broke up the sods rather like a gardener turning his spade in the earth as he digs. The results were for many years controversial but certainly less pleasing from an aesthetic viewpoint than high cut work and less effective in heavier soil. Fields ploughed by a 'digger' seem ragged and untidy, while in traditional horse ploughing neatness was a first essential, as was keeping to a straight line. The semi-digger was a plough of compromise, widely used in practical farming up to the 1940s.

At ploughing matches a level plot is marked out for each team, with dimensions of 80 yd long and 12–14 yd wide. Headlands must be left open and well clear at either end of the furrows so that spectators do not encroach on turning operations or finished work. The use of plots is determined by a draw, held some time before the contest begins. Each plot is pegged out, using official markers and the ploughman's own pegs. Times are set for ploughing each plot with a fair allowance for the teams but no excuse for unnecessary delay. It is, however, unusual for a contestant not to finish his quarter acre well within the given time.

Horses at ploughing matches should always appear well-groomed and harnessed or dressed, there being nothing to gain and much to lose in presenting a

Above *Suffolk geldings ploughing in the 1977 'All Britain Ploughing Match' held at Aldenham in Hertfordshire* (Colin and Janet Fry).

Below *A pair of Shires taking part in a ploughing match* (E. J. Anderton).

Percheron horses dressed for a ploughing match (E.J. Anderton).

sloppy turnout. Preparations must be made well in advance, especially if long distances are to be travelled, which is frequently the case in modern times.

There are different rules in different areas, many concerning the use of helpers or assistants. In some parts there are horse holders, while some ploughmen have a youth or second man to guide the horses. This is frowned upon in other areas and certainly makes the task seem less skilful or a real test of individual ability. The justification for helpers is that modern crowds are frequently noisy and restless, making the horses unsure of themselves. The extra hand is needed to keep the team steady while the ploughman concentrates on the more technical side of his work.

It is essential for any one hoping to win contests to make a good start, which is where the extra hand gives the greatest advantage. The first line must be straight, according to the pegs, which are knocked out as the share passes them. The second ripple or furrow has to be turned-in towards its fellow, the furrow wheel fitting neatly into the furrow groove. There must not be any deviations, second and subsequent furrows lying in close parallel without breaks or cock-ups, the aim being a well-prepared and even seedbed. Following two ripple furrows, also known as scratch furrows, heavier furrows are drawn, made by tilting the plough to one side.

Chapter 10

Still in trade

Introduction

Perhaps the most important work performed by draught horses, or at least running agriculture a close second, was in delivery or cartage services. Even after the coming of steam railways large numbers of horse-drawn vehicles were necessary to carry goods, in both wholesale and retail quantities, between customer, factory and railhead. The ideal, in most industries, was to have private railway sidings or canal wharves, but some firms and small traders could not find or afford sites in such convenient places, while in certain areas the extension of railway tracks was an impossibility. The answer lay in central goods yards or receiving depots and fleets of horse drays, often operated by the railway companies, but sometimes by their agents, running frequent shuttle services. At the other end of the scale nearly every shop and store, in most towns, had a pony or cob with delivery vans to represent almost every line of business imaginable.

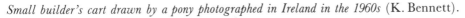

Small builder's cart drawn by a pony photographed in Ireland in the 1960s (K. Bennett).

Left *A Manns dray delivering to the Golden Lion in Wellingborough during the 1970s.*

Right *Whitbread's Shires enjoying a holiday* (Whitbread's Brewery).

Many larger or more important retail outlets had correspondingly larger stables, with fleets of two- or four-wheeled vehicles, often painted in most attractive liveries. These latter varied from the high-roofed, deep-welled pantechnicons of furniture stores and removers, to milk floats, bread vans and the swift, light carts of butcher and fishmonger. Before the age of cheap and universal refrigeration it was essential not to delay or over-expose certain foodstuffs, especially meat and fish, so that swiftly moving ponies with gig-type two-wheelers were frequently seen weaving in and out of slower traffic to deliver lunch-time chops, loaves straight from the oven and Dover soles — the fish often caught and landed the same morning.

Motor vehicles began to take over in the 1930s but there were still many firms clinging to horse transport throughout the Second World War and well into the 1950s. They stayed in some areas longer than others but seemed to vanish by the end of the decade, almost overnight. It was as if a magician had waved a massive wand and banished carts, drays, vans, floats and wagons, not only of the railways, local councils and large haulage firms but of many smaller men depending on a corner shop, street round or market stall. When managers and foremen from various transport departments were pensioned-off, the new and frequently younger men taking their places, perhaps released from highly mechanised war work or military service, soon reduced or diminished the number of draught horses on the pay roll, determined to make a clean sweep with the modern image in mind. The fuel crisis and rapidly rising costs of both repairs and raw materials were then only matters of distant rumour, perhaps beyond belief.

If it had not been for the larger breweries and one or two other astute enterprises draught horses, in the ordinary sense, would have become extinct. Brewers and vintners were traditional supporters of horse-drawn vehicles, from the earliest days. They certainly knew as much, or more, than anyone in trade concerning the value of publicity, not only sending their magnificent teams through city streets but to shows, carnivals and promotions in all parts of Britain and sometimes abroad. It was a brewery that horsed the Lord Mayor's Coach at Newcastle-on-Tyne, with its pair of magnificent Cleveland Bays, while the firm of Whitbreads in London have provided Shire horses for the Lord Mayor's Show and other public festivals for generations.

Brewery horses

It is perhaps fitting to open this chapter with a short survey of Messrs Whitbread's contribution to the life of working horses, based on dignity and tradition as much as profitability. Whitbreads, among the aristocrats of the brewing industry, have used Shire horses for more than two centuries. Samuel Whitbread the first opened a brewery in London about 1742, bringing 30 Shires with him from a farm in his native Bedfordshire, to use in general delivery work. Shire horses are descended from the chargers of ancient warriors who rode into battle, encased in plate and chain armour, seldom moving faster than a slow trot but crashing through the enemy lines more like tanks than conventional war horses of a later period. Their training for battle with its smoke and noise required a sound temperament, so that they were ideally suited in later years for the confusion of city traffic. Most Shires

are powerful and hardy, well able to drag huge loads of beer from pub to pub, often over rough cobbles and badly made roads. In the period before the Great War Whitbreads had extended their business to such an extent that there were over 300 horses at their City depot alone. Here there are now modern stables on two different levels or stories, shared, at one period in recent years, with the City of London Mounted Police.

The original Whitbread drays were two-wheeled trucks with barrels mounted in a crosswise position, the driver or drayman perched on the first barrel. Horses were in tandem pairs or one behind the other, the leader guided by a man on foot known as the trouncer or assistant. When barrels had to be lowered into underground cellars, down steep ramps, this would be done with ropes and chains hitched to the lead horse (also known as the chain horse), when detached from the wheeler or shaft horse. Most modern drays are now four-wheelers, often mounted on pneumatics, drawn by pairs abreast, on either side of a wagon pole. Whitbreads, however, still keep a replica of their original two-wheeler, which appears in street parades and carnivals, attended by men wearing mid-18th century costume with knee breeches and broad-brimmed hats. It may be noted that Whitbreads were pioneers of the 'green grass treatment' which meant sending their city horses to a rest farm, deep in the country, for regular holidays.

Between the world wars motor lorries were brought in to cope with long distance deliveries and horse numbers dropped to between 30 and 40. There are now 16 horses at the Chiswell Street stables in the city, all used in daily work while sharing ceremonial duties at coronations, jubilees and the Lord Mayor's Show. Alfred Munnings PRA, previously mentioned for his painting of 'The Return from Ascot', was a frequent visitor to the Whitbread stables, where he drew and painted many of the horses, both in their stalls and waiting to be sent out with the morning deliveries. The present delivery round is within a five mile radius of the brewery.

Horses used by this firm are bought-in from several parts of the country but mainly from farms in Yorkshire, Lancashire and Cheshire. On one stud farm near Nantwich, which has supplied many replacements in recent years, the animals needed are often chosen as foals and receive their early training — lasting up to five years — on the farm itself. Taken to London in the firm's special horse boxes, they are soon given further training, alongside older and more experienced animals — then matched for colour, height and temperament with a fellow Shire, to become part of a working pair. Although larger teams appear at shows or in street parades the most economical way to work them in daily life is hitched in pairs to a four-wheeled wagon.

Shires weigh in the region of a ton apiece, sometimes slightly heavier, and require a healthy, balanced diet. Special care is taken of both diet and feet. There is a resident farrier or shoeing smith who keeps records of the shape and size of all the hooves in his care, every one of which is slightly different. To keep heavy horses in good condition they must be well fed and the shoes an exact fit, especially when working over hard roads.

Every year the horse teams take part in a hundred shows and publicity events. Just before the running of the Whitbread sponsored Gold Cup at Sandown Park, a pair of Shires from Chiswell Street lead the thoroughbreds to the starting post, an annual tradition greatly appreciated by the cheering crowds. A Whitbread's show wagon and pair of matching greys is frequently the chariot for many carnival and beauty queens in every part of the country. Wherever or whenever they appear they are a constant reminder of the nation's heritage and proud traditions.

One of the go-ahead northern firms to play an important part in the revival of draught horses has been Messrs Daniel Thwaites of the Star Brewery, Blackburn,

Float.

Lancashire. This was mainly the responsibility of David Kay, now a respected higher executive but, during the late 1950s and early 1960s, a Departmental Manager. The horse transport section had been fully mechanised over 30 years earlier, but Mr Kay knew there was still a place for horses both publicity-wise and to save money. He approached his superiors on this subject and spoke with such conviction that he was given a chance to put his theories into practise, a decision which was never regretted. During the winter of 1958-59 there was considerable work of restoration in the stables and stable yard, then used as a fuel store. The premises were virtually reconstructed and are now some of the finest and most up-to-date in the country, tiled from floor to ceiling and provided with the latest in heating, ventilation, drainage and hot and cold water supplies. There is also a special harness room with finely made show harness in dust proof glass cases. At night each horse is comfortably bedded-down in a deep layer of peat moss. It may be noted that although the horses are blacks most have white fetlocks or stockings which tend to stain on straw.

The first Shire was purchased in May 1959 and since then the firm has gradually increased its stud. There are now between six and nine horses in the Blackburn stables at any given time. The black Shires of Daniel Thwaites are not only familiar on the local streets within a mile radius of base, but winning prizes at major shows throughout the country. For many years they were the only firm from the north to represent commercial stables at the Horse of the Year Show in

Shires owned by Daniel Thwaite's Brewery, Blackburn (Wally Talbot).

London. A charming depiction of them appears in a street mural painted on the end wall of a house almost facing the main entrance of the Star Brewery, in the centre of Blackburn. During the summer months two of the horses are nearly always on tour publicising the firm, winning honours and keeping the name of their owners before the public. This could not be done with the largest and most expensive motor vehicles, as for every passer-by caring to give lorries a second glance, hundreds will flock to see a drive-past of stately Shires.

It was the opinion of Mr Kay, by whom the author was granted an interview at his Blackburn offices, that on selected journeys the horse drays were much cheaper than motors. A lorry costs far more to buy initially and the horse remains in work for many years after the machine is nothing but a load of scrap metal. Up to a certain age the value of a good horse increases and although it declines after that age is reached it is always worth something — at least more than a clapped-out motor lorry. Within a mile or two of base the horse, even in modern traffic, is faster and more efficient than a lorry, all this having been proved and double-checked by the 'stop-watch bandits' or work-study groups.

A pair of geldings from the Star Brewery can deliver upwards of eight tons of beer per day to local pubs and clubs. Although the firm formerly used a modern-type dray, low-slung and riding on pneumatics, Mr Kay greatly prefers the traditional vehicle with wooden spoked wheels and steel rims, which he claims are lighter and usually easier to handle. Fortunately there are still good wheelwrights in the area so that repairs present no difficulties. Many other firms still using horse-drawn wagons have changed to disc wheels and pneumatics because they are easier to repair and replace, without expert assistance, than spoked wheels.

Staff in the brewery stables are fairly easy to replace, with the right training, and for every post advertised there is always a surplus of applicants. It is now a policy of the firm to keep a register of likely persons involved. Like the horses of many other concerns, Thwaites' Shires have an annual holiday, sent to rich pastures in the nearby Ribble Valley. After several appearances on television they have made friends not only in the town and show ring but nationwide. People frequently send them Christmas parcels with gifts of carrots and lump sugar, although perhaps forgetting the stable staff and draymen who do so much to make the enterprise successful. One of the assets of a commercial stable is the high price of manure, which makes a considerable contribution to upkeep.

Horses are often real characters and Mr Kay records how one of their Shires, although hard-working and normal enough in other respects, appears to dread the white patches on zebra crossings — which it seems to think might be hollow or insubstantial, only walking on the black stripes. Another horse refused to pass a certain pub without stopping, it being discovered that the landlord's wife had frequently given it carrots and other tit-bits. All the horses are admired and respected wherever they deliver or make an appearance. They are rarely involved in mishaps of any kind and there have been no public or private complaints concerning them. Motorists, especially the drivers of large commercial vehicles, are usually courteous and prepared to give way, especially when horses are seen to be leaving the yard to enter or cross the main thoroughfare.

A pair of grey Shires from Tetley's Brewery (Tetley's Breweries).

In handling horses on a busy road traffic dangers are often over-rated, serious as they may be for all road-users. If or when trouble occurs with horses it is either a fault in training or because the driver has taken fright. According to an old Spanish proverb 'fear travels down the reins' and the most stolid animals loose their nerve if the person on the box goes to pieces. Horses that were used for shunting in busy railway stations could be trained to work or rest without batting an eyelid, surrounded by steam locomotives that looked and behaved in a far more alarming manner than even the largest motor vehicle, but only because they had been looked after by persons unlikely to show panic themselves.

On the opposite side of the Pennines in Leeds, the brewery of Josua Tetley and Sons Limited, still keep a stable of eight working horses — all Shires. There have been Shires with Tetley's for over 150 years and may be there for many years to come. Joshua Tetley, the founder of the firm, like many a good Yorkshireman, was a great enthusiast for the heavy breeds, a tradition long respected by his successors. A few years ago it was suggested that the horses should be banned from the streets of the city centre for their own safety and the good of other road users. The next day over 1,000 letters poured into the office of the Yorkshire Post, begging and demanding that the horses should be kept. There were no exceptions brave enough to sign their names — whoever made the suggestion would have been unwise to continue his argument.

Some people claim that horses are stupid but, if anything, their reactions are sometimes quicker than those of human beings. They are certainly easier to handle at traffic lights than cars or lorries, having taught themselves to relate the click of a time switch (unheard by most humans) to the sequence of lights, bracing for the off a vital second before the actual change.

The mixed greys and bays of Tetley's Brewery deliver beer over the often steep gradients of Leeds within a radius of five miles of the brewery. This is in the nature of hard work and it has been estimated that horse shoes weighing 6 lb are lifted clear of the ground every second, proving that a Tetley Shire moves 308 tons per eight hour shift. On a regular delivery stint a brewery horse is shod every three weeks. Some of the animals are over 18 hands high and weigh nearly a ton each, being able to draw three times their own weight. Most horses work in the drays until they are 14 or 15, after which they are sent to the country and end their days in light work. The decision for semi-retirement, however, is only made after a thorough examination by a skilled veterinary officer.

A pair of Tetley greys have appeared in the City of London, at the Lord Mayor's Show, hauling a smart delivery dray with white-walled tyres. They also appear in the parade at the Annual Shire Horse Society Show in Peterborough, and at many other shows in Yorkshire and the North of England. Show preparations take hours of scrubbing, polishing and grooming but, considering the public reaction, are well-worth the effort.

Also on the eastern side of the Pennines is the Tadcaster Brewery of Samuel Smith and Sons, famous for their Tadcaster Ale and as suppliers to Her Majesty's Armed Forces. They claim to be the oldest commercial brewers in Yorkshire and now have the only eight horse team of matching grey Shires in the world. There are ten horses or five matching pairs, used mainly for publicity purposes but also for short-haul deliveries. They do not deliver every day but are well exercised in town streets, most of the deliveries being in autumn and winter. The entirely new and purpose-built stables are directed by Colonel Agnew, an ex-cavalry officer. Each box is provided with a manger, hay net and automatic drinking bowl. Routine commences at 6 am, when the first feed is offered. Mucking-out, cleaning and grooming follows and the horses are presented for work or exercise at 9 am. The second feed of the day is at 11 am, with a third feed at 4 pm and a last feed at 9 pm. Feeds consist of bucketsful of bran to which scoops of flaked maize, chopped hay and a little molassine meal is added. Hay nets are filled three times a day, any residue being returned for use as 'chop' (chopped hay). The head horseman, Tom Gibson, prefers wood-shavings for bedding as they are cleaner than straw and not so likely to be eaten by the horses, who frequently pluck straws wound into the long hairs of their fetlocks. All the horses are well-matched greys in the region of 17 to 17.2 hands high.

Members of the public wishing to see the stables are taken on a conducted tour,

Eight horse team of grey Shires owned by Samuel Smith and Sons, Tadcaster Brewery (Samuel Smith and Sons).

starting with the tack room, where they may inspect the trophies and see the harness being cleaned. They are then taken through the forage stores and into the stables proper, to inspect the Shires at close quarters. The firm have now published a small book or pamphlet on their stables, which may be purchased from the Old Brewery, Tadcaster, at the cost of £1.50 per copy.

Messrs Adnams of the Sole Bay Brewery, Southwold, Suffolk, returned to horses in 1970. They had previously given up their stud through loss of grazing in the East Coast floods of 1953. There are at present five Percherons, all geldings, mainly working between the brewhouse and distribution centre on short runs for which lorries would be inadequate and far more expensive. Special drays have been constructed for the purpose, each taking five tons of cask beer on pallets, which are easy for loading and unloading. There are 14 trips per day of five tons each, with return empties. A single horse and separate dray are kept for town deliveries and to a pub on the foreshore which can only be reached over stretches of shingle. Although Adnams do appear at shows and festivals their stable is essentially for working horses. It is reckoned, however, that a considerable amount of publicity is earned while the horses and men are carrying out their ordinary tasks. At present horses are purchased from commercial breeders but the firm is hoping to establish its own stud-farm in the not too distant future. Percherons are preferred as they are smaller than Shires and easier to handle, although capable of the hardest work when required. They stand better than Suffolks while loading and waiting, and do not tend to loll or fall about.

Horses are stabled in loose boxes near the brewery. Much of the hay and straw they use is grown in fields or on parcels of land attached to country inns, originally for the use of publicans, many of whom once kept a small amount of livestock, but no longer required by them. Mr J. Adnams has long been an admirer of Percherons, even before they were used by his firm. In 1978 he was elected 79th President of the English Percheron Breed Society.

At Young and Company's headquarters in Wandsworth, London, known as 'The Ram Brewery', there are now 20 Shires, 14 of which are used for deliveries and the rest for showing and publicity. More than 30 of Young's houses have their supplies delivered by horse transport, usually in pair-horse wagons or drays. It is claimed, as by several other brewers, that horses are more economical than lorries over short distances and have the added advantage of attracting public attention at the same time.

The Ram Brewery stables, although surrounded by streets and buildings, in a busy part of south London, has all the appearance of a rural venue. There is a blacksmith's forge, wagon repair shop, horse exercise yard and forage stores, the country atmosphere greatly enhanced by poultry pecking about for grains of corn

Percherons owned by Adnams, Sole Bay Brewery, Southwold (Adnams Brewery).

Background photograph *Eight horse team of black Shire geldings owned by Messrs Young's Brewery, Wandsworth, South London* (Colin and Janet Fry).

Inset *Pair horse deliveries in London by Young's Brewery of Wandsworth* (Fleet Fotos).

Above *A Shire owned by Young's Brewery* (Fleet Fotos).

Left *A pair of Shires on a delivery round for Wadworth and Company of Devizes* (Marcher Lithographies).

and even a few ducks, familiar in many farmyards up to the 1950s. In the harness or tack room are displayed more than 1,000 cards recording the cups and prizes won at horse and agricultural shows throughout Britain. Young's horses, like those of Daniel Thwaites, are blacks with white stockings and fetlocks. These are the official colours of the St John's Ambulance Brigade and some of the horses have turned-out on their behalf at certain parades and charity shows, especially the annual Tulip Festival at Spalding, Lincolnshire. A few of Young's horses have also been used for funerals although not being the traditional type associated with the so-called 'black brigade'. There is an exciting programme of shows and social events at which they appear each summer season.

At one period, during the 1960s, Mr J. A. Young, then a busy executive, engaged the services of a time and motion study team. This was to make a survey of activities in the brewery as a whole, although members of the group almost collapsed in fits of laughter when forced to make way for a team of working Shires. Yet on examining facts and figures they soon changed their minds and recommended the retention of such transport, at least for short hauls. With more horses taking beer to local pubs costs were soon pulled back to what they had been ten years earlier. Youngs are bound to have faith in the excellence of their products as each of their horses imbibes at least a quart of ale per day.

In the South West of England, Wadworth and Company of Devizes have also gone back to horse deliveries in recent years. They were greatly assisted in this enterprise by the counsel and friendly interest of Mr David Kay of Thwaites' Star Brewery, previously mentioned. There was also considerable practical assistance from a Mr R. Gifford of Corsham in Wiltshire, whose family have bred and trained draught horses for many years. A start was made with a pair of bay Shire geldings, each with an almost identical white blaze down the centre of the forehead. They were introduced in 1974 and a second pair added some months later.

The horses are mainly used for daily deliveries within a radius of $1\frac{1}{2}$ miles of the Northgate Breweries, although taking part in the odd horse show or carnival in season. Ten months were spent in preparations before the horses arrived, as old and unsafe buildings had to be replaced by a new all-wooden stable block (supplied by Messrs Fredericks) with four boxes and two tack or harness rooms. Some harness was acquired from another brewery in Hull, while other sets were made by Colin Knapp of Brockenhurst, Hampshire. The appearance of pair-horse drays on the streets of Devizes certainly adds to the colour of an ancient market town, long famed for the quality of its ales, a tradition nobly upheld by the house of Wadworth.

Some of the most interesting brewery turnouts in Britain are now operated by Messrs Vaux in the North East of England and in Edinburgh where the same company owns Lorimer's Brewery. These are mainly Percherons, like the horses of Adnams, but with a few Gelderlanders for lighter work. There is a stable of 17 horses at the Sunderland headquarters, made up of 12 Percherons and five Gelderlanders. The Gelderlanders are of Dutch origins, imported from the Netherlands. They all work throughout the year, within a five mile radius of the

Above *Harnessing up in the morning outside the Vaux Brewery stables* (Robert A. Smith).

Below *A rest en route to the Durham County Show* (Robert A. Smith).

Above right *'Zorki', a Gelderlander from the Vaux stables, delivering wines and spirits* (Robert A. Smith).

brewery, saving at least one-third of the operating costs of motor vehicles on town streets. Far from being a nostalgic gimmick they are kept for sound reasons of economy, although it must be admitted that beyond a certain range motor transport is superior. Percheron-hauled drays make two deliveries per day of between two and three tons, while the Gelderlanders handle two loads of 30 cwt per day.

The firm of Vaux have run a brewery in Sunderland since the early part of the 19th century. They were moved, however, from their Union Street Stables in 1875, when the North Eastern Railway Company needed to build the present Central Station. The brewery then adopted a new location in Castle Street, where it has been ever since. The business was taken over on the death of the founder by two brothers, Major Cuthbert and Colonel Ernest Vaux. Ernest Vaux is remembered in modern times as serving with Lord Baden-Powell in South Africa and helping him to found the Boy Scouts Association, an early Boy Scout Troop being allowed to camp on land owned by the Vaux family at Grindon near Sunderland. Up to the period of the Second World War Clydesdale horses were used for delivery but were gradually replaced by steam wagons and motor vehicles. There were eventually only two horses left, kept for salvage work and dumping rubbish.

After the Second World War, with a problem of increasing town traffic, it was decided to replace the Clydesdales with Percherons. These often have better temperaments than other heavy horses and were much quicker than Shires, in the personal experience of their handlers. Clydesdales are an active but highly-strung type of animal, especially in noise and bustle, needing the firm hand of a young but experienced horseman, a type not always available in modern times. As the costs of motor vehicles shot up by leaps and bounds in the post war world, it was found necessary to increase the stud and return to horse deliveries, at least in the short-haul context. This is only part of the attraction as the sight of grey Percherons on the streets, in working gear, thrills most people as they pass by.

The Vaux Percherons are mostly geldings but with one or two mares. Stallions are no longer kept at Castle Street and the last foals were bred in 1962. Most Percherons are born black or dark brown, but turn grey or dapple-grey towards their prime. An older horse may be almost pure white but acquires rust-coloured spots or freckles in extreme old age. Some turn grey early while others stay black, a colour now greatly favoured in Canada and the United States, where the breed has always been popular. In France a few are bay or chestnut but these colours are, for some reason, frowned upon by the English Breed Society.

Apart from delivery work the Vaux Percherons are exhibited at all the major shows in the North of England, with repeated success. They make an annual appearance at the Durham County Show, held in Lampton Park, to which the whole stud frequently travels in convoy, making a wonderful sight for any lover of horses or animals, who might happen to be passing. They have several times won silver cups at the Royal Show for the best commercial turn-outs. They are in great demand at local shows, carnivals and during the University Rag Week. At Christmas they draw Santa Claus in procession, through the town centre, to his grotto at a local store.

The Gelderlanders are all chestnuts, being the special pride of Major Douglas Nicholson, who retired from the Chairmanship of the Company in recent years. Major Nicholson was the son of Sir Frank Nicholson who married the daughter of John Story Vaux. He served with a unit of Yeomanry-cavalry known as the Scottish Horse throughout the Second World War, which was later absorbed into the Royal Artillery. He was a highly skilled whip and frequently drove the Gelderlanders to a private road coach, well to the fore in driving competitions at international level. He has now been succeeded in the firm by his son Paul, who also drives and is more than likely to uphold a family tradition. Vaux horses, especially the Gelderlanders, are well-known in Continental countries. In 1972 Major Nicholson drove them to win the Gold Medal of the World Driving Championships, held in Munster, Germany. At Budapest he was placed third in the first European Driving Championship Rally. During the Silver Jubilee of 1977 the Vaux team drove from Buckingham Palace to the Mansion House where they picked up several distinguished passengers, and took them in procession to St Paul's Cathedral, returning to the Royal Mews at night to stable the horses.

Although a few of the traditional drays and wagons are still used for show purposes, most of the working vehicles are of modern design, purpose-built and running on pneumatic tyres. There are also nine-barrel horse tankers delivering draught beer and lager to the cellars of public houses by means of piped connections.

Preparing for a Saturday morning dip in the sea (Robert A. Smith).

The Vaux horses are fed at half-past six in the morning and receive a second feed at 8 am, before starting the morning deliveries. They return for a mid-day meal at noon, then take out afternoon beer, returning at half-past four for the second grooming and an evening meal of oats, bran and chopped hay. Water and salt licks are always available in each stall. The average horse gets through 1 cwt of hay per week. In winter and cold weather a mash is served warm with added molasses. Straw is used for bedding and amounts to 2 cwt per horse per week. Saturday is a half-day in stables and all horses are given an extra grooming before bedding-down in the early afternoon. In summer there is frequently a Saturday bathe in the sea, which is enjoyed almost equally by men and horses. No deliveries are made on Sunday, which is a day of rest. All the horses are given a fortnight's summer holiday in pastures at Hasting's Hill.

All harness is cleaned and saddle-soaped each day, as soon as it is taken from the bodies of the horses. This helps to keep it not only smart and supple but prevents dangerous cracks that may lead to snapping and breakdowns.

At the time of writing the Brewery have no intention of discontinuing their support of draught horses, either heavy or light. This is certainly a happy and progressive stable, where everyone seems to fully understand his place in the scheme of things. The dozen or so drivers and their assistants do their utmost for the horses, both in and out of stables, by whom their kindness is well repaid by

A four horse team of Percherons from the Vaux stables (Colin and Janet Fry).

years of loyal service. Most horses are now bought direct from stud farms at the age of three or four years. They work at least ten to twelve years before retiring. A pair of Percherons costs slightly less than the Gelderlanders but very much less than a motor vehicle, which would not last nearly so long, without costly maintenance. The Percheron is usually a healthy animal and requires very little attention apart from feeding, grooming and shoeing. No vehicle tax is levied on horse-drawn transport.

Some of the most interesting horse teams working on the Continent represent the Carlsberg Brewery of Copenhagen, Denmark. This internationally famous firm still has a stable of 18 working horses, all of the Jutland breed. Shorter and more compact than English Shires, their colouring resembles that of the Suffolk Punch being chestnut or sorrel with lighter manes and tails. They pull a type of beer wagon which is long and low-slung, in the Continental style, with barrels not only placed on top but hanging from the underside of the loading platform. Several similar vehicles and teams are still to be seen in parts of Germany, Switzerland and Central Europe. In Canada the Carlsberg brewery is represented by an associated firm making use of a traditional vehicle and team, although drawn in this case by Belgian draught horses. Harness and paintwork is in an attractive mixture of red, green and silver, which are the Carlsberg house colours.

In the United States of America considerable use is made of heavy horses, especially for promotional work. Among the more outstanding examples are two magnificent eight-horse hitches of bay Clydesdales, known as the 'Budweiser Horses'. They feature in many street parades and at State Fairs, also appearing in the film 'Hello Dolly', drawing an American-type beer wagon with raised sides and patent 'Sarven' wheels. These are owned by the Anheuser-Busch Incorporated Brewing Company, which is now the world's largest commercial brewery. They are based on St Louis, Missouri, although one team, touring in the east, is frequently kept in New England. Until the early 1970s there was only one hitch but this proved so popular that a second hitch was called into being, at public demand. At the time of writing a third team is in preparation. Both teams are on the road ten or eleven months of the year, travelling over 40,000 miles in three special horse boxes. There is an average 325 engagements per year.

Other horse-drawn deliveries

Turning from breweries to house removals, it is interesting to note that Messrs Abels of East Anglia, based on Norwich Road, Watton, Norfolk, still keep a stud of six Shire geldings. These are mainly used for promotional work, although sometimes making token or local deliveries. They make frequent use of fields and paddocks owned by the company, where they also engage in seasonal harrowing and rolling. Abels are engaged in removals both in the British Isles and abroad, frequently employed on behalf of the armed forces of the Crown and for Government Departments. What might be termed the flagship of their van fleet is a recently restored pantechnicon built in 1903 and sometimes drawn by three

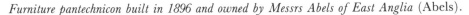

Furniture pantechnicon built in 1896 and owned by Messrs Abels of East Anglia (Abels).

Above *A token delivery made by Coalite to one of their oldest customers* (Coalite).

Below *The stables of the Solid Fuel Advisory Service, Lichfield* (Rackhams of Lichfield).

horses abreast. There is also a furniture van of 1896 and a miller's wagon, the latter shown to a single horse. All the horses are dark bays. A few other firms in the removal business also use pantechnicons for advertising but usually hire or borrow horses for their show-work.

The Coalite Group based on Chesterfield also keep Shire horses, a pair being stabled at Mansfield Woodhouse in Nottinghamshire. They are used mainly for publicity work but this frequently involves deliveries linked with promotions, in different parts of the country. A typical example was a turn-out in connection with the opening of a new 'Fireside Shop', dealing with solid fuel products, at Heanor, Derbyshire. The agent in question asked 'Coalite' to deliver supplies to his customers of the longest standing, by whom this patent fuel had been ordered on a regular basis for a matter of fifty years. Coalite have done extremely well in the show ring, winning 46 first prizes in 1983 alone, events including the Royal, Great Yorkshire and the Royal Norfolk shows.

The Solid Fuel Advisory Service has seven Shire horses, stabled on the aptly named Shires Estate, Lichfield, Staffordshire. There are also five other Shires in semi-retirement at Middlesbrough, Stoke-on-Trent, Beverley and Stafford. The Board represents an association of the main coal producers and sales organisations in Britain, including the National Coal Board, the Co-Operative Fuel Trade Association, Rexo, Coalite Limited and several other groups. Their aim is to encourage the use of smokeless solid fuel in the domestic context, through promotions and publicity, for which Shire horses are an admirable media. They appear in parades, carnivals and at horse shows, also making a certain number of regular deliveries throughout the local area in winter. They are kept in loose boxes and looked after by a number of highly efficient young women, their stables being purpose-built in modern surroundings. The largest horse in the stud, all of which are now grey geldings, is 'Hobart Long John' who is the tallest Shire in England and perhaps in the world — 19.15 hands high. A new show wagon with equirotal wheels and pneumatic tyres cost £6,000, ordered from a Walsall firm in 1981, while a far more attractive vehicle (in the author's opinion) of traditional design, was sold in 1929 for £17.

Before and during the Second World War one of the sights of London was an omnibus or Brougham-type delivery van, working for Scott's the Hatters of Regent Street, driven to a smart, high-stepping hackney. The top-hatted driver and groom had just the right touch of style and elegance, even appearing in several films based on life in the West End. It was a great disappointment to many when this turn-out was taken off the road, although its place has since been occupied by several other vehicles almost as beautiful, one delivering scent and another connected with a fashionable restaurant. These both are single horse vehicles.

Perhaps the most elegant of the larger delivery vans, also known as a 'coach' is owned by Rothman's, the tobacconists of Pall Mall. It was formerly a private or station omnibus and is 120 years old. Drawn by a pair of grey horses of the hunter type it is used daily in the streets of London, making deliveries to embassies, clubs and restaurants, covering about 70 miles per week. During the summer it appears

Omnibus van.

at a number of horse shows and non-equestrian social or sporting events. During
the 1983 show season Rothman's team won six major prizes in the ring and two
championships — the latter at Doncaster Pageant of the Horse and at Newbury.
The vehicle is most striking in its present livery of scarlet and black with white
lettering. When redecorated it receives at least 17 coats of paint and four coats of
clear varnish. Harness is of black patent leather with highly polished brass
fittings, made to shine like silver. There are four horses in the company stables,
although the eldest, known as 'Kelly', has recently gone into retirement on an
Essex farm. The stables at Elvaston Mews, South Kensington, are a great
attraction, especially to tourists, holiday-makers and foreign visitors.

It would be impossible to mention or describe every firm or individual still
using horses for deliveries in Britain, although regretfully some of the better
known concerns have relinquished not only their horses but also the traditional
service of door-to-door delivery rounds. A number of retail items involved are no
longer required, or are now sold in such a way that deliveries cease to be practical.

Omnibus van owned by Rothmans of Pall Mall (Rothmans of Pall Mall).

Less coal is needed with so many smokeless zones, although a Bridlington firm of factors is still flourishing at this well-known seaside resort, totally dependent on its gentle giants. Milk and bread are still known to be delivered by horses in parts of Northamptonshire, although the majority of traditional milk floats and bread vans — once common-place — have now disappeared into limbo, perhaps ending their days as garden sheds or hen-coops. An excuse for reducing or limiting deliveries made by one firm was that so many housewives are now at work for the greater part of the day, dropping in at the corner shop or supermarket, to buy off-the-shelf, on the way home. Others use the boot of the family car and the fridge-freezer to buy in bulk and stock-up well in advance, all of which discourages the use of delivery vans.

In many of the larger towns of Australia, milk is still delivered twice a day, using heavy horses such as Clydesdales and traditional floats. The driver or 'Milko' is employed on a piecework basis, according to the number of bottles he delivers. In most suburbs he runs between the houses, dropping off pints by the

Coburg bread van.

Morning call.

armful while his horse follows on a parallel course. This could not be done economically with a petrol-driven or electric truck, plus an assistant to share the spoils.

In the modern idiom most deliveries are now tied-in with publicity and special needs, although enthusiasts must be thankful for a sight of vehicles that still exist and the number of shows at which there are commercial classes to support them. A fair selection of the remaining totters (scrap dealers), street hawkers or barrow boys may still be seen at the Greater London Horse Show and the Essex Tradesman's Show, with the vehicles and horses used in the London area and the Home Counties.

Chapter 11

Odd jobs

The title of this chapter may seem slightly misleading as it relates to spheres of work at one time widespread and almost commonplace but now dwindling to rare or minority interests. Mining is a case in point as, at one time, over 70,000 horses and ponies were used underground in British collieries alone. These are now reduced to a mere handful with about 25 in South Wales. The majority are in the North East of England serving the pits of Durham and Yorkshire. The size and type of animal varies with dimensions of shaft and gallery, also depending on local mining methods. In the north and Scotland, Shetland and Icelandic ponies of small, compact build were always preferred, while in South Wales large Cobs and Cob/Shire crosses of the vanner type were frequently used, ponies in name only. The larger Cob-type has also been found useful in drift mines of which there are

Left *'Darkie' at Big Arch Pit, Talywann, South Wales.*

Right *Clydesdale geldings working for the Aberdeen District Council in 1983* (Clydesdale Horse Society).

still a fair number in private ownership, in Eastern parts of South Wales and Gwent. Drift mines are not entered down a vertical shaft by means of a lift or cage, but through a tunnel-like cavern in the side of a mountain.

The animals remaining underground are kept for maintenance and repair work, able to squeeze into small, awkward places. They have always been well-treated and were great favourites with the handlers and miners in general. Most have regular holidays in meadows on the surface and the idea that pit ponies automatically went blind after a certain period, is without serious foundation. In most of the larger collieries, especially under the National Coal Board, the stabling was always sound and there were expert vets and farriers to care for average needs. When ponies are pensioned-off or made redundant they are sold to good homes and not left to the tender mercies of shady dealers. Even the hours worked are governed by the strict regulations of the 'Pit Ponies' Charter'.

At one period every corporation and municipal authority had large numbers of horses, mostly Shires, assisting with rubbish or salvage collection, helping to keep the streets clean and hauling gigantic water carts or even tar-boilers for road repairs. They were known as 'Vestry Horses' as their upkeep and well-being was greatly determined at meetings of local councillors in church halls and vestries, especially before the days of local council offices. Numbers began to dwindle during the late 1950s although a few towns, especially north of the border, have seriously considered their full-time reinstatement. Glasgow and Fife are only two of these places although perhaps the most heartening revival has been in the

Left *Hackney.*

Below right *Mr Leslie Colloby with his landaulet, used for weddings* (T. Edgson).

'granite' City of Aberdeen, now a boom centre for North Sea oil and a modern city in every meaning of the word. Aberdeen leads the way where others may be expected to follow.

A total of 12 Clydesdales are now employed in the streets and parks of Aberdeen, replacing numbers of lorries and vans. There may be many arguments concerning the economics but their value, in terms of public goodwill and as a tourist attraction, are beyond measure. The Leisure and Recreation Department of Aberdeen Corporation also runs a four-in-hand stage coach, known as 'The Sheffield Telegraph', used both for hire to clubs, groups and individuals and to take parties of tourists or school children on sight-seeing expeditions. It is drawn by a team of grey Cob mares, that were previously used in town haulage work. It is anticipated that working costs and maintenance will be covered by income to show small profits. Hackney carriage licence plates, approved by the area Public Carriage Officer, are fixed to the bodywork.

Still within the realm of Scotland there are a number of ponies of the Highland breeds still used to carry dead stags in the sport of deer stalking. This is not perhaps as popular a pastime as in former days, which means that fewer ponies are needed, although no reasonable substitutes can be found for the remainder. The Highland pony, not unlike a small cart horse, can be ridden and driven, being up to remarkable weights and ideal for pannier or pack work. It is extremely sure-footed and able to survive on land that would not keep a deer, sheep or mountain goat, much less the average horse. There are now two distinct breeds, derived from common stock — a pony of the Western Isles known as a Barra and a pony of the mainland known as a Garron. Both are fine animals but the Garron is larger and heavier. Towards the end of his reign King George V frequently rode a grey Highland pony on his estate at Sandringham.

There are now a number of people, perhaps with one or two carriages and a pair of horses, who hire them out for weddings and other social occasions. They are to be found in or near several large towns or suburban areas, perhaps combining this work with other commitments such as promotional work or running a riding school. Mr Leslie Colloby of Northfields Farm, Hampton-in-Arden, midway between Birmingham and Coventry, although now in semi-retirement and carrying on his business as more of a hobby than a full-time occupation, is perhaps a typical example. At his Warwickshire farm, so near one of the largest urban areas in Britain, he has several carriages including a Victoria, a landaulet and a wagonette-phaeton, which may be hired for long or short periods. Mr Colloby drives from the box, frequently attended by a friend and associate, also a noted horse breeder and breaker, both wearing Victorian style liveries. The horses are a pair of chestnut geldings, both of which are a cross between an Arab and a Welsh Cob. There is also a Welsh Cob mare, slightly smaller but of excellent conformation, reserved for the phaeton. Mr Colloby has also used the mare for light farm work, including chain harrowing in awkward places, where tractors would find it difficult to turn. The horse and vehicles will travel several miles to a venue but are

Right *Mr Leslie Colloby with his Welsh Cob mare and a wagonette-phaeton* (T. Edgson).

transported in a special box and trailer, so that they arrive as fit and fresh as possible. Their normal work is to convey the bride and groom from church or registry office to the place of reception. Often there are several trips ferrying members of the family and guests of honour, perhaps taking the happy pair to station or airport on the first stage of their honeymoon, or as a token trip. The most popular vehicle is the Victoria with its low sides and half-hood, in which the bride's dress may be seen to full advantage.

A far more unusual job for a horse is to help keep open a national footpath. The West Yorkshire County Council now employs a horse and sledge for repairs on the main route of the Pennine Way, in places where wheeled vehicles are unable to approach within two miles. The horse, named 'Bobby', is owned and worked by a local farmer but on loan to the County Council, while the Countryside Commission subsidise his hire and upkeep. 'Bobby' is frequently used in dragging loads of stone, timber and hard core for the repair of walls and footbridges; he is stabled near the footpath, for easy contact and access, at Hebden Bridge.

In Bristol it is now possible to ride on a sight-seeing tour through cobbled streets of the original dockland area. This may be done in an improvised horse bus of the single-decker type, owned and driven by a Mr Coleman. The vehicle was purpose-built and takes a payload of 25 passengers seated on the crosswise or toast rack principle. The vehicle is drawn by a single horse of medium-heavy draught type. There are two horses on the strength, each used in turn for a basic run of 12 miles per day. The trip lasts about 20 minutes.

Also in Bristol the 'Avon Friends of the Earth', an important conservation group, have organised an interesting and profit-making salvage scheme. Its street-to-street waste paper, cardboard and old bottle collection is aimed at

making people conscious of the valuable trees saved by such measures, and of the need for conservation in general. It is conducted entirely by horse-drawn vehicles which is said to cut the cost of collection to one-seventh of the three motor lorries that were otherwise needed. The team of ten is directed by Rosemary Windmill, a qualified Instructor of the British Horse Society. There are 20 collection days each month amounting to over a ton of paper per day, which is sold to local mills at a fair price. Profits are ploughed back into the work and other similar schemes are planned in places as far apart as Newcastle and Plymouth. This also saves the rate-payers a great deal of money as destroying or incinerating waste by public authorities is an expensive process. It would not be a success without horses and carts which not only cut the running costs but attract necessary attention and prove firm favourites with people of all ages and from most social groups.

Perhaps one of the most incredible uses for the modern horse is launching lifeboats, which is still done in parts of Holland. The boat is dragged down to the beach, ready manned, and lowered into the surge from a carriage-like structure mounted on huge artillery wheels. This was frequently done in Britain and many other European countries during the Victorian era and there are wonderful stories of horses leaving the shelter of lonely pastures, on hearing a maroon or signal gun fired, to stand in readiness near the lifeboat station. One elderly horse continued to do this even after retirement, dying of a heart attack in his last attempt to answer the summons. On the island of Ameland in the northern part of the Netherlands the lifeboat is drawn over 2 km by medium-heavy Gelderlanders from a nearby farm. They time the signals perfectly and are usually waiting to be harnessed by the third blast of a siren. Eight horses are used for the actual launch, with four attached on each side.

Chapter 12

Warning and Advice

This short chapter is mainly addressed to those who contemplate using horses and vehicles for profit or pleasure, especially in connection with advertising, transport projects or promotional schemes. Running a horse bus for seaside visitors, hiring out carriages for weddings and this type of thing all have their attractions and seem good fun. Some might consider them interesting time-fillers or an easy way to make a living, but they would be quickly disillusioned, especially if they lack previous experience. These projects are hard work for a knowledgeable person and only worth considering, first time out, with a partnership or loyal assistant, sharing the responsibility.

It is not just a case of any old horse suiting any type of cart or carriage available. Apart from the inhumanity of expecting uncomplaining creatures to pull loads beyond their capacity there are also matters of taste and tradition worthy of far more than passing thought. Many hiring and local transportation projects have failed through sheer ignorance of what is required or may appeal to the more discerning members of the public. Sloppy turnouts, the gaudy colours of the funfair and vehicles that appear thrown-together or badly designed for their work, tend to repel rather than attract. Making the right effort in the right way has an effect on positive thinking and will not only fire the imagination of would-be customers but percolate through to horse and driver.

To acquire the right approach and not be lumbered with a horse-bus that seems suspiciously like a second-rate delivery dray, needs taste and understanding, only approached through experience, observation, reading and visits to places where horse-drawn vehicles are still kept and used. Do not be ashamed to ask questions and challenge opinions, above all have a clear idea of what is needed, both in attending auctions and ordering something new. Yet this can only be done when the would-be purchaser knows something about vehicles, their style and purposes. Too many have walked into a factory or workshop asking to be provided with something to run up-and-down the promenade and ended up with not just a 'horse-killer' but an insult to both taste and intelligence. Unless one is aware of these problems there is no point in dealing with horses and carriages and would be far better off with a well-proportioned motor vehicle or electric truck.

Wheels that are too large or too small for the actual wheelbase, diminutive show wagons hauled by mighty Shires or lumbering arks dragged by weedy ponies, betoken little more than greed or folly. Buy the best one can afford, keep it in good trim and take the advice of proven experts, especially in the early days. See that a vehicle is not only in fair running order but thoroughly safe and highly presentable. Painting and repairs, greasing and oiling should never be neglected, while the horse must have sufficient work, rest, food and caring consideration. This is not just sentiment or even common sense but a guide to success and all-round satisfaction.

Appendices

1 Types of Horses

The types or breeds listed below are mainly related to those mentioned in the text and is not intended to be a complete guide.

Arab   The oldest thoroughbred horse in the world, which has influenced most existing stock. Renowned for its combined beauty, hardiness and docility. Originated in Arab countries of the Middle and Near East, but now bred in all parts of the civilised world, especially Poland. With other eastern breeds it is known as a warm or 'hot blood'. Noted for the proud carriage of head and tail also for a small muzzle and dished or concave profile of head and face. 14.1 to 15 hh.

Ardennes   Draught horse of mountain breed, widely used in agriculture and forestry. Particularly used in Sweden and now gaining popularity on British farms. Cheaper to feed and easier to handle than most of the heavy breeds. About 15 hh.

Boulonnaise   Medium draught horse of Northern France, used for fast, light work. 16 to 17 hh.

Brabant   Heavy Belgian horse, widely used for agricultural work and heavy haulage. Also known as the 'Flemish' or 'Belgian draught horse'. 17 hh.

Breton   Medium French draught horse with clean legs. A quality animal with many thoroughbred ancestors. The 'Postier Breton' is an even finer but slightly smaller horse, used for coaching, found in the interior. 15 to 16.2 hh.

Carmargue   Grey horse of the Carmargue in the South of France. Used for cattle herding and as a cavalry troop horse. Noted for its large head and long back. 14 to 14.2 hh.

Cleveland Bay   An English breed of great antiquity, noted for its fine conformation and dark bay colouring with black points. Used as a carriage horse and for light agricultural work. Now widely popular in the Royal Mews for ceremonial duties. Bred in the Cleveland Hills of North Yorkshire and County Durham. 15.2 to 16.1 hh.

Clydesdale   The heavy draught horse of Scotland and the borders. First bred in Lanarkshire by crossing local mares with Flemish stock, also influenced by the English Shire. Quick and alert but of less certain temperament than the Shire. Usually bay or brown with splashes of white, white stockings and either black or white fetlocks. Used for both farm work and heavy draught in industrial areas.

Very popular in Commonwealth countries settled by Scots. Around 16.2 hh.

Dales   Ride or drive pony, formerly used as a pack animal. Noted for its hairy legs and described as a miniature cart horse. 14 to 14.2 hh.

Fell   A slightly smaller and more refined version of the Dales Pony. Found in the Lake District and on the western slopes of the Pennines. Used as a pack horse and for light agricultural work. 13 to 14 hh.

Gelderlander   Medium weight coach horse, also used for farm work. Can be ridden or driven. Bred in the Dutch province of Gelderland. 15.2 to 16 hh.

Hackney   Modern descendant of the roadster or Norfolk Trotter. Later improved by crossing with Arab and Thoroughbred stock. Used both for light carriage work and smart delivery rounds. Noted for smart appearance and exceptionally high action. 14.3 to 15.3 hh. The Hackney Pony is a smaller version, mainly kept for show purposes and known as the 'Bantam Hackney'. 14.2 hh and under.

Hafflinger   Austrian mountain pony, widely used in all parts of Europe for light agricultural, pack work and forestry. A deep chestnut colour with flaxen mane and tail. 14 hh.

Hanoverian   German carriage horse, also popular in liberty acts of the circus. 16 hh.

Highland   There are two main types, known as the Garron and the Barra. Both are popular for light agricultural and pack work. The larger Garron is used to carry the bodies of slain stags in deer stalking. The mainland Garron is 13.2 to 14.2 hh while the island Barra is 13.2 and under.

Holstein   German medium draught and carriage horse. 16 hh.

Irish Draught   Used for riding and light agricultural work, also as a carriage horse. 15 to 17 hh.

Jutland   Ancient breed of heavy draught horse, widely used in Denmark. Usually a chestnut colour with lighter mane and tail. May have been influenced by the Suffolk Punch. 15.2 to 16 hh.

Knabstrup   Danish breed of dual purpose animal, used for riding and light draught work. Covered with small leopardlike spots it is ideal for circus acts. 15.3 hh.

Lippizzaner   Carriage and riding horse frequently trained for high school acts. Noted for an impression of combined grace and strength. The horses of the Spanish Riding School at Vienna are traditionally stallions of this breed. 15 to 16 hh.

Morgan   Versatile ride and drive horse of North America. Capable of ploughing, timber hauling and harness racing. 14 to 15 hh.

Norwegian   Small draught horse or pony mainly used in farming and forestry. There are two main types, both duns or creams with black eel or dorsal stripes. The older breed, from coastal regions, may be descended from the war horse of the Vikings. The slightly larger horse of the interior is now more numerous. 14.1 to 14.2 hh.

Oldenburg   A strong, versatile light draught horse of Western Germany, which may also be ridden. The largest of the warm-blooded breeds, descended from Arab stock. Frequently used as a military charger. 16.2 to 17 hh.

Orlov   Russian carriage horse, also used for trotting or harness racing. First bred by Count Orlov, during the mid-18th century. About 17 hh.

Percheron   French agricultural and coach horse, also widely used for military purposes. Noted for its considerable infusion of Arab blood. Large numbers were brought to England, shortly after the First World War, greatly admired for its combined willingness and hardihood. Perhaps the most widely distributed draught horse in the world popular in Japan, Canada, the United States and many countries of Europe. Almost clean legged. The stallion is 16.3 and the mare slightly shorter.

Quarter Horse   American saddle horse first bred by early settlers in the southern states. Frequently competed in quarter mile sprint races through forest clearings. Ideal for ranching purposes. 15.1 to 16 hh.

Shetland   Small but hardy pony bred in the Shetland Islands to the north of Scotland. Originally a small pack and agricultural animal but later used in the coal mines. Ideal for circus and pantomime, also as a child's first pony. Height is measured in inches rather than hands. They should be 42 inches when fully grown.

Shire   English heavy draught horse of great courage and strength. Descended from the War Horse or Great Horse of the Middle Ages, but greatly improved during the 18th century. Used for both agricultural purposes and town draught. Noted for a high head carriage, Roman nose and large amounts of feather or fetlock. Weighs a ton and capable of moving five. In the region of 17 hh but many are now even larger.

Suffolk Punch   Heavy horse of East Anglia, always a shade of chestnut with lighter mane and tail. It has a more refined appearance than most heavy draught horses and was greatly improved by the blood of trotters and thoroughbreds. Noted for strength, courage and docility. It will pull until falling to its knees. Its clean legs and low-slung body make it ideal for ploughing and cultivation. 16 hh.

Thoroughbred   More correctly the 'English Thoroughbred'. A quality horse now mainly used for sporting purposes. Descended from one of three eastern sires, imported during the late 17th and early 18th centuries. Now much faster than the Arab but lacking the combined endurance and fine temperament of its ancestors. About 16 hh.

Trackenher   Light-medium carriage horse of Eastern Germany. 16 hh.

Welsh Cob   Hardy and sure-footed, general purpose animal, suitable for riding, driving and pack work. Originally bred in West Wales. Has a certain amount of feather or fetlock on the lower limbs. 14 to 15 hh.

Westphalian   Warm-blooded riding horse of West Germany, descended from Arab stock. Bold and hardy, now bred mainly for show jumping. 15.2 to 16.2 hh.

2   Glossary of terms relating to horses, harness and vehicles

Axle arm   The outer extremity of an axle on which a wheel is fitted.

Axle tree   Central beam or block forming part of an under carriage, to which axle

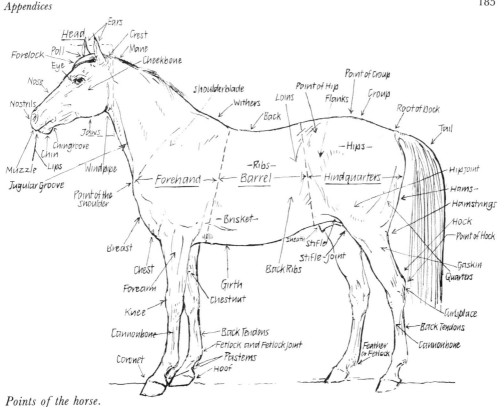

Points of the horse.

arms are fitted. Also a support for the continuous axle.

Bay   Horse of a medium to dark brown colour, often with black points.

Blaze   White stripe or marking down the centre of a horse's face.

Blinkers   Also known as 'winkers' and 'blinders'. Leather eye shades fitted to the bridle of a draught horse to prevent it seeing the object it draws at the rear. Not worn in some countries or by more reliable horses.

Box   Driving seat on a horse-drawn vehicle, frequently above a form of tool box, where valuables were also kept.

Breeching   Rearward harness straps in horizontal form, holding back the load of a draught horse on steep hills.

Bridle   Leather headstall of strapwork, forming attachment for reins, bit, etc.

Brood mare   Mature female of the equine species, capable of breeding.

Car   Small, light passenger vehicle, eg, Rally Car.

Carriage   Large, usually four-wheeled passenger vehicle of the open type. Also the under gear on which the body of a vehicle rests.

Carriage part   Any part of a horse-drawn vehicle excluding the bodywork.

Cart   Two-wheeled vehicle usually for goods or agricultural produce. Those used by passengers were of inferior quality or cheaply made, eg, tub cart.

Cart gear   Heavy harness for attaching a horse to a cart.

Chain horse   Horse working in chain gears rather than shafts or leather traces. Often worked in tandem with a shaft horse.

Clean legged   Draught horse without much feather or fetlocks on its limbs.

Chestnut   Horse of a reddish-golden colour *or* horny growth on the inside of the leg.

Coach   Large enclosed or headed vehicle. Ran on four rather than two wheels. Seldom drawn by a single horse.

Coachman   The driver of two or more horses from a box seat.

Collar   Either a neck or breast collar. Part of harness fitting round the neck and shoulders, taking the strain of draught and forming attachments for traces, etc.

Colt   Young, male horse.

Dog stick   Sprag or rearward projection attached to the axle tree of a large vehicle to prevent it running backwards downhill.

Drag shoe   Also known as a 'drug-shoe' or 'drugbat'. A wedge or slipper fixed under a rear wheel to prevent it over-running the team on a steep hill. Acts in reverse of the dog stick.

Draught   The ability of a horse to draw its load.

Draught horse   A horse bred and trained to draw loads, rather than a riding horse.

Driver   Person driving or controlling a single draught horse.

Eel stripe   Back or dorsal stripe appearing on certain breeds of horse.

Ex-bed   Axlebed or base forming part of the under-works of a wagon.

Feather   The hairy fetlocks of many draught horses.

Felloes   Pronounced 'fellies'. Outer segments of a wooden cart or carriage wheel, at its rim or circumference, forming outward attachment for the spokes.

Gelding   Castrated male horse. More docile than a stallion.

Hammercloth   Protective covering over a box seat, partly decorative.

Hitch   The number of horses attached together for draught *or* a vehicle and its draught team combined.

Ladder   Projecting framework at the front or rear of a vehicle to support its load.

Leader   One of the forehorses of a team, not directly attached to a vehicle.

Lights   The windows of a coach or enclosed passenger vehicle.

Lock   The turning circle of the forecarriage on a vehicle.

Mare   Mature, adult female of the equine species.

Naff   Outward projecting part of a wheel hub. Also known as the naff-end.

Perch   Longitudinal support under the bodywork of certain vehicles.

Pole   Longitudinal bar or beam forming attachment for wheel horses drawing large vehicles.

Riding machine   Gang plough or other farm implement driven from a fixed seat.

Roller bolt   Upright attachment shaped like a mushroom, on the front of a large vehicle, to which traces are attached.

Shaft   Less frequently known as a 'thill'. Side bars usually in pairs, forming attachment for draught horses at the front of a vehicle. May be single or double but usually the former.

Shaft horse   Horse between shafts, harnessed next to the vehicle it is intended to draw.

Splinter bar   Horizontal bar at the front of a large vehicle to which roller bolts are fixed.

Steersman   Person operating a horse-drawn farm implement by walking alongside. Not always in charge of the horses.

Swingletree   Horizontal bar at the rear of a coach horse, forming attachment for traces, etc.

Tailboard   Also known as a 'tailgate'. End-board or boards at the rear of a cart or wagon. May be lowered and raised for loading or unloading purposes.

Thoroughbraces   Longitudinal suspension of certain heavy vehicles, in the form of toughened leather straps.

Turn-out   Combined horse and vehicle ready for work or show.

Wagon   Originally spelt 'waggon'. Large, four-wheeled vehicle used for agricultural and commercial purposes, ie, Harvest Wagon, Farm Wagon, etc.

Wagon standard   Upright metal brace at the side of a wagon forming a support for the side-planks or bodywork.

3   Places to visit

Aston Scot Working Farm Museum, Church Stretton, Shropshire.
Arlington Court near Barnstaple, North Devon.
Bass Museum of Brewing, Horninglow Street, Burton-on-Trent, Staffordshire.
Bath Carriage Museum, Circus Mews, Bath, Avon.
Bristol Industrial Museum, Prince's Wharf, Bristol, Avon.
Camborne Carriage Museum, Lower Grillis Farm, Treskilland, Redruth, Cornwall.
Cotswold Farm Park, Guiting Power, Nr Cheltenham Spa, Gloucestershire.
Courage Shire Horse Centre, Cherry Garden Lane, Maidenhead Thicket, Maidenhead, Berkshire.
Cricket St Thomas West Country Wild Life Park, Chard, Somerset.
Devon Shire Horse Centre, Dunstone, Yealmpton, Near Plymouth, Devon.
Dorset Heavy Horse Centre, Brambles Farm, Edmondsham, Verwood, Near Ringwood, Dorset.
Douglas Horse Tramway, Douglas, IOM.
Gawsworth Hall, Macclesfield, Cheshire.
Guinness Museum, St James's Gate, Dublin, Republic of Ireland.
Hereford and Worcester County Museum, Hartlebury Castle, Hartlebury, Nr Kidderminster.
Hull Transport Museum, 36 High Street, Hull.
Industrial and Social History Museum, Forth House, Kirkcaldy, Fife.
Ipswich Museum, High Street, Ipswich, Suffolk.
Leicester Museum of Transport and Technology, Abbey Pumping Station, Corporation Road, Leicester.
London Transport Museum, Covent Garden, London.
Merseyside County Museums, William Brown Street, Liverpool City, Merseyside.

Museum of East Anglian Life, Abbots Hall, Stowmarket, Suffolk.

Museum of Lincolnshire Life, Burton Road, Lincoln.

Museum of Transport, Albert Drive, Glasgow.

Norfolk Shire Horse Centre, West Runton Stables, West Runton, Cromer, Norfolk.

North of England Open Air Museum, Beamish Hall, Nr Stanley, Co Durham.

Nottingham Castle Museum, Nottingham.

Preston Hall Museum, Preston Park, Eaglescliffe, Stockton-on-Tees, Cleveland.

Raby Castle Museum, Staindorp, near Darlington, Co Durham.

Science Museum, Exhibition Road, South Kensington, London SW7.

Scunthorpe Borough Museum, Oswald Road, Scunthorpe, South Humberside.

Spinney Farm, Home of the Shires, Tilley Lane, Windmill Hill, Herstmonceux, East Sussex.

Staffordshire County Museum, Shugborough Hall, Great Haywood, Nr Stafford.

Sussex Shires, Haremere Hall, Etchingham, East Sussex.

Tolson Memorial Museum, Huddersfield, West Yorkshire.

Transport Museum, Matlock, Derbyshire.

Transport Museum, Witham Street, Newtownards Road, Belfast, Northern Ireland.

Tyrwhitt-Drake Carriage Museum, Archbishop's Stables, Mill Street, Maidstone, Kent.

West Yorkshire Folk Museum, Shibden Hall, Halifax, West Yorkshire.

Whitbread Hop Farm, Bettring, Paddock Wood, Kent. (Holiday home of the Whitbread Shires.)

York Castle Museum, Tower Street, York.

Yorkshire Museum of Carriages and Horse Drawn Vehicles, York Mills, Aysgarth Falls, Hawes, North Yorkshire.

Bibliography

Care and Showing of the Heavy Horse by Edward Hart, Batsford, London, 1981.

The Harness Horse by Edward Hart. Shire Publications, Princes Risborough, 1981.

The Heavy Horse, Its Harness and Decoration by Terry Keegan. Pelham Books, London, 1973. Fourth impression 1978.

The First Hundred Years by Harry Constantine. Douglas Corporation, IOM, 1975.

Princes of the Plough by B. Cockroft. J. M. Dent, London, Melbourne and Toronto, 1978.

Gentle Giants Ralph Whitlock. Lutterworth Press, Guildford and London, 1976. Second impression 1979.

Collecting and Restoring Horse Drawn Vehicles by D. J. Smith. Patrick Stephens, Cambridge, 1981. Paperback 1984.

The Royal Mews Buckingham Palace by Sir John Miller, Pitkin Pictorials, 1981.

The English Farm Wagon by J. Geraint Jenkins. Oakwood Press for Reading University, 1969.

The Elegant Carriage by Marylian Watney. J. A. Allen, London and New York, 1961. Reprinted 1979.

Horse Power by Marylian and Sanders Watney. Hamlyn Publishing Group, London, New York, Sidney and Toronto, 1975.

Salute the Carthorse by Maj The Rev P. A. Wright. Ian Allan, London, 1971.

English Horse Drawn Vehicles by David Parry. Frederick Warne, London, 1979.

Discovering Horse Drawn Carriages by D. J. Smith. Shire Publications, Princes Risborough (third ed), 1985.

Discovering Horse Drawn Commercial Vehicles by D. J. Smith. Shire Publications, Princes Risborough (sec ed), 1985.

Buses, Trolleys and Trams by Charles A. Dunbar. Weidenfeld and Nicholson, London, 1967.

All Drawn By Horses by James Arnold. David and Charles, Newton Abbot, 1979.

Index